SACRAMENTO PUBLIC LIBRARY

3 3029 03182 6191

D0430036

OCT 1994

THE
BEER ENTH
GUID

TASTING & JUDGING
BREWS FROM AROUND
THE WORLD

GREGG SMITH

A Storey Publishing Book

STOREY

Storey Communications, Inc.
Schoolhouse Road
Pownal, Vermont 05261

Jeffery
"Don't Give up the Ship"

Edited by Christine P. Rhodes
Cover design by Carol J. Jessop
Cover illustration by Mary Rich
Text design by Meredith Maker
Text production by Leslie Carlson
Line drawings by Christine Erikson
Indexed by indi-indexers

Copyright © 1994 Gregg Smith

All rights reserved. No part of this book may be reproduced without written permission from the publisher, except by a reviewer who may quote brief passages or reproduce illustrations in a review with appropriate credits; nor may any part of this book be reproduced, stored in a retrieval system, or transmitted in any form or by any means — electronic, mechanical, photocopying, recording, or other—without written permission from the publisher.

The information in this book is true and complete to the best of our knowledge. All recommendations are made without guarantee on the part of the author or Storey Communications, Inc. The author and publisher disclaim any liability in connection with the use of this information. For additional information, please contact Storey Communications, Inc., Schoolhouse Road, Pownal, Vermont 05261.

Printed in the United States by BookCrafters
First Printing, February 1994

Library of Congress Cataloging-in-Publication Data

Smith, Gregg, 1952–
    The beer enthusiast's guide : tasting and judging brews from around the world / Gregg Smith
                p.   cm.
        "A Storey Publishing book."
        Includes bibliographical references and index.
        ISBN 0-88266-838-2
        1. Beer.   II. Title.
    TP577.S59   1994
    663'.42 — dc20   93-14117
                                                                    CIP

ACKNOWLEDGEMENTS

With special thanks and appreciation for all the support
from my wife Carrie and daughters Darcy and Jessica.
In addition, the support of Mom and Dad;
brothers Rick, Paul, Karl, sister Leslie
and their spouses Jackie, Leona, and Glen.
Also for the help from my co-brewers
Jack, Lorraine, Joe, Lisa, and Michael.
Acknowledgements for review and additional
information in this book go to Beer Judges:
John Naegle, Keith Symonds, Carrie Getty and
Lisa Variano, and all the members of the
New York City Homebrewers Guild.
Special thanks for help in review
of commercial samples to Bill Mayew,
Pete Kokolakis, and Ben Stevenson.

TABLE OF CONTENTS

HOW TO USE THIS BOOK

This book is about beer and the concept of quality. As a beer enthusiast, you have already developed a taste for quality beers rather than an appetite for quantity. This book will help you to understand what characterizes good beer style, by evaluating characteristics ranging from aroma and appearance, to taste and body.

It is amazing to discover, during this learning process you are undertaking, that beer, such a seemingly simple beverage, is actually quite complex. From the basic ingredients of water, hops, barley, wheat, and yeast, the brewer can fashion over 70 distinct styles of beers. Although you probably won't like each style, you should become well-versed in each of them in order to become a knowledgeable beer enthusiast. In addition, the advanced evaluation techniques discussed in this book will provide you with an excellent reference both during your educational process and after you have received your judging certification.

In Chapter 1, you will learn about the brewing process and the brewhouse design. Chapter 2 explains the basics of converting grain into beer. Understanding these procedures is important, since the brewer's manipulation of ingredients is what enables him or her to impart unique characteristics to different styles. Chapter 3 addresses beer styles in terms of aroma, feel, color, and taste, using the terminology you learned in Chapter 2. Here, you learn to compare commercial samples to the general standards for your favorite German pilsner, imperial stout, brown ale, and virtually every style.

Chapters 4 and 5 explain the language of beer and the vocabulary needed to converse with other beer judges. The terminology used to describe both a beer's attributes and its faults are reviewed in detail.

For those aspiring judges, Chapter 6 outlines the Beer Judge Certification Program, run by the American Homebrewers Association and the Home Wine and Beer Trade Association. Included in Chapter 6 is more information on ingredients and their effect on the beer profile. Judges must be able to identify what characterizes proper beer style, and, in the case of faults, the causes and corrective actions that should be taken to improve the beer.

Readers who have already passed the judges' exam will find the book an unmatched ready-reference for continuing training and a valuable tool for judging. The chapters on styles and characteristics help the judge to provide consistent feedback to brewers.

Do not let any of the technical information in the book overwhelm you. We are all in a process of continuing education, and, although judges are expected to know a certain amount of this technical information, they do not have it all memorized. The styles, descriptions, and guide to tasting is information that I have written to help you to become an experienced evaluator and consumer of all types of fine beers from around the world. *Prosit!*

CHAPTER 1

BEER AND THE STORY OF CIVILIZATION

We have all heard the phrase "accident is the mother of invention," and in the world of beer, the cliché certainly holds true. In order to understand the accident as it relates to beer, imagine traveling back in time to when the Mediterranean was the seat of civilization. At this time, barley flourished and was a dietary staple. Barley was cultivated successfully due to the climate in the Mediterranean and was used as the basic ingredient in breads, cakes, and other common food products. A farmer during that period discovered that if barley was allowed to get wet, germinate, and eventually dry, the resulting barley product would be sweeter and would also be less perishable than the original barley had been.

We can imagine this "unfortunate" incident step by step. The farmer probably found that his barley crop had been wet. To salvage the barley which he worked so hard to cultivate, the farmer tried to spread the barley out to dry. Most likely, germination had already begun, and the grain had therefore malted and developed a much sweeter taste. The sweet result of what the farmer considered a disaster was what we today call malted barley. This malted barley was probably a huge success, since it would contribute a much sweeter taste to breads, cakes, and anything which had previously been prepared with unmalted barley.

Since barley malt became such a common ingredient, we can further speculate that, at some point, a loaf or bowl of this malt became wet, probably inadvertently left out in the rain. When damp, the dissolved starches and sugars in the malted barley became susceptible to wild yeast, which may have lit on the sweet mash and started spontaneous fermentation. The owner of this new mix of mash and yeast probably discovered, upon tasting, that the mix actually tasted quite good. Without realizing the impact of his discovery, this ancient farmer brewed the first beer.

You may think that this scenario is unlikely, but take into consideration the amount of time that the owner had spent planting, caring for, and harvesting his barley crop. With this in mind, you can be sure that he would not simply toss away the new mixture without finding some way to try to use it. This experimentation with the mixture of malt and yeast has set the groundwork for beer and brewing. And, in fact, as unlikely as it may sound, several scholars have suggested that this is precisely the way in which beer was discovered. A few bold historians will even go so far as to suggest that the cultivation of barley for the purpose of making beer is what made people actually settle in one area and learn about selective seed propagation, study agriculture, begin the development of calendars, and make important historic discoveries that framed civilization.

Historians can confirm the suggestion that beer has been

Evidence of the existence of beer as seen in hieroglyphics and pictograms dating back to the earliest days of civilization.

common since the earliest days of the civilized world. Through existing hieroglyphics, pictograms, and written records, it is evident that early Babylonians studied the different types of barley in 6,000 B.C. In the artifacts of ancient Mesopotamia, there is evidence of the brewing and consumption of beer written on clay tablets which are said to date back to 4,000 B.C. The name of their brew was Sikaru, or grain wine. They even had a goddess of brewing, named Nin-Bi. In Mesopotamia, as well as in Egypt, artifacts show the baking of barley loaves which were then crumbled in water to make beer. Indeed, Sumerian pictograms went even further by publishing what is considered to be the first beer recipe. Later, the Romans colonized what is now Europe and, in the process, they introduced the making of both beer and wine to the people. The Roman word for beer, "Cerevisia," is a Latin root, derived from Ceres, the goddess of agriculture, and "Vis," the Latin word for strength.

As time passed, the production of beer came under the watchful eye of the Roman Church, as commonly happened with other early experimental sciences. Above the doorway of an old monastery in Rome is the well-known inscription, "In heaven there is no beer, that is why we must drink it here."

There is even a patron saint of brewers, Saint Arnou, Bishop of Metz, who died in 640. In 641, a procession was reportedly carrying his body for interment in Metz, when the caravan stopped for a rest in the village of Champigneulles. With regret, the townspeople are said to have had only one mug of beer to offer. The legend tells us that a great miracle took place when all drank from the single mug which, despite all those partaking in the drink, did not go dry. Another saint, a monk from Ireland named Saint Gall, is credited with being the first modern brewer. He brought new methods of brewing from the Celts to the Abbey that was the center of Charlemagne's empire. Subsequently, Charlemagne listed brewers among the tradesmen that district administrators should employ.

In time, monks, as beer's first researchers and tradesmen, refined the methods of brewing, but there was still very little known about the role of yeast in completing fermentation. Because of the uncertainty in the process, one of the earliest symbols for brewers was a six-pointed star, the symbol for alchemy. Alchemists, of course, were best known for their vain attempts to change lead into gold. The mysterious art of brewing was equally regarded as the miraculous feat of transforming water into a magical drink. In fact, the star symbol can still be spotted on beer labels today.

Hops, or *Humulus lupulus,* was also a known cooking ingredient as far back as the Roman times. A member of the *Cannabis* family, hops were used in brewing by religious orders as early as the 800s. By the fifteenth century, there was a record of hops used in Flemish beer imported into England,

and by the sixteenth century hops had gained widespread use as a preservative in beer, replacing the previously used bark or leaves.

Royal patronage of brewing was formally established in the thirteenth century by Duke Jean I, "Jan Primus" of Brabant, Belgium. He is honored throughout Europe as the so-called King of Beer. Legend portrays him as the founding father of the Knights of the Mashing Fork, purported to be the first brewers' guild.

By 1420, German brewers had started to make beer by lagering, which means "to store." Brewing was not possible in the warm months because wild yeasts prevalent in the warmer weather of summertime would sour the beer. Brewers discovered that brewing in the cold months and storing the beer in caves in the nearby Alps imparted a stability to the beer and enhanced it with a cleaner taste, although they did not know why. Today we know that the reason the beer was clearer and cleaner was due to the fermentation process the beer underwent in the cold, during which the chemicals and bacteria responsible for clouding or hazing beer were unable to thrive and were therefore filtered out of the beer.

Perhaps the most widely known event in brewing history was the establishment of German standards for brewers. The first of these regulations was decreed by Duke Albert IV in 1487. This was the inspiration for the "Reinheitsgebot of 1516," which is the most famous of beer purity laws. Established by William VI, Elector of Bavaria, this pledge of purity states that only four ingredients can be used in the production of beer: water, malted barley, malted wheat, and hops. Yeast, though not included in this list, was acceptable, as it was taken for granted to be a key ingredient in the brewing process. The "Reinheitsgebot" was the assurance to the consumer that German beers would be of the highest quality in the world. Thus, the purity law acknowledges the European disdain for adding adjuncts such as corn, rice and any grains other than barley and wheat as well as cheap sugars to the beer. Ironically enough, this German purity law was abolished in recent years, allowing German brewers to use adjuncts, in order to compete with American brewers who are mass-producing their lighter beers and out-selling European brewers in their own markets in some instances. Despite the law being revoked, German brewers have chosen to stand by the purity law and risk fewer sales due to the expense and time involved in brewing a superior product.

The next great development occurred in the mid-nineteenth century, through work done by Louis Pasteur, the first to propose an explanation of how yeast worked. Shortly thereafter, samples of Bavarian yeast provided by the great Munich brewer Gabriel Sedelmayer to the Carlsberg brewery were studied by Emil Hansen, head of the laboratory. Hansen was successful in identifying a single-cell and strain of the bottom-fermenting lager yeast. Coinciding with this discovery was the new glass-making technology which prompted a switch from the old ceramic style mugs to glassware which highlighted the bright, clean, gold traits of lager beer. It is no wonder lager was soon the rage throughout Europe, with the rest of the globe not far behind.

Beer can even be credited with a role in the settling of America. In the log on the Mayflower, the Pilgrims entered a passage explaining their decision to land at Plymouth Rock: "Our victuals have been much spent, especially beer." Today in America, one wonders why, with all the great beers in the world, the United States has developed a taste for a thinner, lighter beer style. At one time, brewing in America embraced many local styles. There were, for instance, approximately 2,400 U.S. breweries operating in 1880. Today, there are over

375 breweries, over 300 of which are microbreweries and brewpubs. The change in taste can be traced back to the era of the Volstead Act of 1919. This Eighteenth Amendment to the Constitution ushered in Prohibition. During this time, the smaller breweries lay idle as the larger establishments limped by with the production of cereal malts and near-beers. Following Prohibition came World War II, with corresponding food shortages and therefore increased substitution of adjuncts for malt. A lighter beer resulted. With a large part of the male population off fighting the war, the work force in America was made up largely of women. Marketing to this war-time population solidified the hold of a lighter-styled beer and, following the war, the large national breweries catered to the tastes of this expanded beer market.

Today, there is a revolution in America as brewing returns to its roots, and a great variety of high quality beers are being revived, due largely to the emergence of over 300 successful microbreweries and brewpubs which are creating remarkable quality beer styles from around the world. Perhaps one day the popular tastes will dictate a complete return to the small regional breweries of old.

CHAPTER 2

THE BREWHOUSE AND BREWING

The conventional brewhouse is designed to take advantage of the benefits that gravity has to offer the brewer. With this in mind, brewhouses are generally multi-level designs, with the brewing process starting on the upper-most level and finishing on the lowest, coolest level. The grain is usually stored at the upper level and, as the process progresses through its various stages, the grain passes through the equipment sequentially to the bottom level of the brewhouse. This multi-level design allows the brewer to actually separate the brewing steps by level, or floors, visually and structurally organizing the entire brewing process.

Aside from understanding the structure of the brewhouse, it is vital for the true beer enthusiast, taster, and judge to understand the key components in the brewing process: malting, milling, mashing, brewing, cooling, fermentation, racking, and finishing. These areas are covered in detail in this chapter.

MALTING

Malting is the process of getting the barley ready for brewing. Each step of the malting process unlocks the starches hidden in the barley, while minimizing haze and off-flavors. In most instances, this task is completed for the brewery by a malster who specializes in this type of work. A description of the malting procedure, including temperatures for each step, is outlined in this section.

Steeping — Here, grain is added to a cistern or vat along with water and allowed to soak at 60°F. The purpose of steeping is to increase the moisture content of the grain to approximately 40–45%. During the 40–hour steeping period, the water is changed periodically (usually three times) to prevent any wild bacteria on the husks from starting fermentation. At the conclusion of the steep, the vat is drained and the grain is transferred to the *germination room*.

Germination — Now, the grain is spread out on the floor of the germination room, where the temperature is maintained at a damp 60°F. In order to understand the germination process, it is important to have an understanding of the anatomy of the grain itself. The *husk* is the protective covering for each individual grain. The thickness of the husk and the amount of husk present varies with each type of grain. The husk is important since it forms the filter bed during the lautering phase of the mashing process. The husk is also a detriment to brewers, since it can be responsible for harsh flavors and tannins, which cause haze in a final product. The *acrospire* is the formal name for the embryonic plant which grows inside the husk during the germination process. The *embryo* is the growing part of the grain, which, if the process were not halted during germination, would grow into a new plant. The *endosperm* is the non-living part of the grain which contains the starches or sugars and proteins or nutrients used by the yeast for fermentation.

During the 5 days following the spreading out of the grain in the germination room, rootlets will begin to form and the acrospire will start to grow inside the husk. Air is blown through the grain from below, since oxygen is needed for germination to occur. The grain must be turned over several times to prevent the tangling of roots and to aid in the oxygen supply. The germination is complete when the acrospire has grown to about ¾ the length of the grain and the endosperm has turned from hard to mealy. The goal of germination is for the starches within the grain to break down into shorter lengths. This is accomplished naturally as the embryonic plant is preparing to grow. At the completion of this phase, the grain is termed *green malt*. This modification of the starches from longer to shorter lengths is important since long chain starches and proteins are not utilized at all in the brewing process, while shorter lengths are very useful in the process. Fully-modified malt can reduce the likelihood of chill haze and is therefore quite a valuable ingredient for brewers.

Kilning—Following germination, the green malt undergoes an oven-like kilning, or temperature drying. In the kiln, the temperature is slowly raised over the course of 30–35 hours. Throughout kilning, the temperature increase must be gradual in order to ensure that the enzymes in the grain are not damaged. The kiln temperature will come to a controlled maximum of 122°F. for lager malts and slightly higher for other types of beers. After kilning, the result is a finished malt, with soluble starches and developed enzymes. The various types of kilned malts are: pale malt, mild ale malt, and high-kilned lager malt. As their names imply, the pale malts are brought to a low-kiln temperature and retain maximum enzyme diastatic power. Mild ale malts are kilned to a slightly

THE BREWING PROCESS

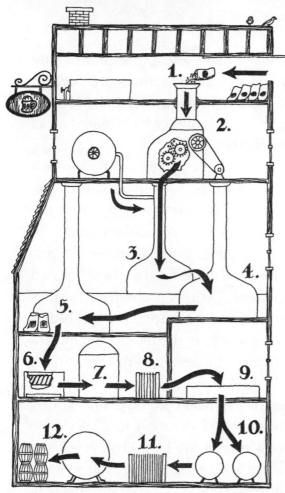

1. Malt is fed into the mill.
2. The mill grinds the malt into grist.
3. The grist is fed into the mash tun, where it is mixed with warm or hot water. If the infusion method is used, only the mash tun is utilized.
4. If infusion is not used, it is during the decoction phase of the brewing process that the mash is sent through the lauter tun, where the mash is clarified and becomes the refined wort.
5. Hops are added to the wort in the brew kettle, where the actual brewing of the mixture occurs.
6. The hops are removed from the mixture, and the wort passes through the hop back flavored by the hops, but clarified.
7. The whirlpool removes the undesirable proteins by centrifugal force.
8. The wort moves through a cooling area, the heat exchanger, where it is brought down to a temperature suitable for fermentation. (See the specific style information contained in chapter three for these temperatures and specifics, since it varies widely from style to style.)
9. The yeast is added to the wort in the fermentation tank or vessel.
10. Following fermentation, the wort moves along to the conditioning tanks, where it sits undisturbed until it reaches its finished, aged state, again variable depending upon the style.
11. The finished beer is filtered here. Note that in order to impart some unique characteristic, some styles are not filtered at all.
12. The beer passes to a holding tank, where it remains until it is bottled or kegged for transport, sale, and consumption.

higher temperature than pale malts and produce a deeper color in the final brew. Higher temperatures are used to produce the high-kilned lager malts, which are rich in aroma and full of body. Commonly used types of high-kilned malts are Vienna Malt and Munich Malt.

Some styles of beer require special types of malt which impart distinct flavors. These malts, sometimes called specialty grains, are produced by deviating slightly from the standard malting procedure. Stewed or mashed malts, for instance, go through the common malting procedure but, before kilning, the grain is sealed in a vat and the heat is raised to near mashing temperatures. At this point, the enzymes convert to sugars. Vents are then opened and the kiln heat is raised further. This process results in the intentional incomplete conversion of the sugars. Those sugars that remain are complex and non-fermentable. They add a unique sweetness and body to the beer. Carapils is a pale-colored grain made by stewing the malt and heating and drying it to a moderate temperature. This process retains the light husk color and non-fermentable sugars that add to the fullness of the light-colored beers which utilize carapils. Crystal or caramel malt is yet another variety of stewed malts. The process of creating crystal malt starts in the same manner as it does for carapils, but finishes with a higher kilning, which deepens the husk color. This temperature also darkens the inner grain by caramelizing the sugars. The result is a reddish hue and a distinct sweetness, smoothness, and body not found in beers made without crystal malt.

Roasting grains undergo the traditional malting process, without being stewed, and are then dried. After the drying process, the grain is exposed to much higher kiln temperatures, which darken the husk and the interior of the grain. The control of time and temperature determine the final color and flavor of the grain. The caveat for brewers is that roasted grains, although adding subtle underlying flavors that are desirable, also can easily add undesirable astringency because of their husks. It is suggested that the roasted grain be mashed with diastatic malt to hasten the breakdown of sugars and minimize the mash time, which decreases the amount of tannins in the beer. (A discussion of diastatic power can be found in Chapter 5, page 82.) There are three major types of roasting malts: brown malt, chocolate malt, and black malt. Brown malt is kilned at a very high temperature using an open hardwood fire. This grain imparts a toasty, roasted flavor. Chocolate malt is drum-roasted and contributes a nutty, chocolate toasted flavor to dark beers. Black patent grain imparts a sharp, burned flavor and is used primarily to add color, since larger quantities can result in an undesirable grainy, bitter astringency in the beer.

MILLING

After the barley has been prepared for brewing in the malting step, it is ready for milling. The typical brewhouse arrangement starts at the top floor with the milling of the prepared grain. Milling is the cracking or crushing of the grain which the brewer has chosen for the particular batch of beer. It is a controlled procedure which should break the grain while keeping the husk itself as large as possible. Proper milling allows maximum yield and minimal amounts of polyphenols or tannins that can cause astringency and haze. On the top floor of the brewhouse, the malt is fed into the grain mill. A typical grain mill is constructed of a set or sets of adjustable rollers, and the distance between these rollers can be set by the brewmaster to crack grains of various widths. Milling the grain allows the grain to absorb the water it will be mixed with, in order for the water to extract sugars from the malt. The grain mill is usually a separate room or floor in the brewery, so that the bacteria that thrive on the dust of the milled husks will not contaminate the product.

MASHING

The milled grain will drop into warm water in a large cooking vessel called the *mash tun*. Mashing converts the starches, which were released during the malting stage, to sugars. In this mash tun, the grain and water mix to create a cereal mash. Because water is such a vital part of this brewing process, the water itself becomes a key ingredient. In particular, the pH of the water and grain mixture, or the mash, is incredibly important in the brewing process, so it is vital that a brewer be aware of setting the proper pH. pH is a measure of acidity of water and is measured on a scale of 1–14. On this scale, 7 is the neutral point. Low pH levels indicate acids present and high pH levels indicate the presence of bases or alkalines. The brewer's objective is to adjust the pH to a range of 5.0–5.8. The ideal value of 5.3 is the most common point in the effective ranges for the *alpha* and *beta amylase* enzymes that break down starches to sugars and the *proteolytic* enzymes that reduce proteins. The measured addition of calcium is one commonly employed method of quickly dropping the pH to the desired level. (See Chapter 5, Brewing Ingredients, for more detail on water and pH.)

The second and more traditional method is the use of an *acid rest*. This step occurs by holding the mash at approximately 95°F. where complex salts in the malt will naturally settle the pH to about 5.8. This value is needed for optimum enzyme activity. The disadvantage of an acid rest is the possibility of increasing the levels of polyphenols. Pale malts and other high-kilned varieties inactivate what is called the *phytase* enzyme, which drops pH. It may take a long period

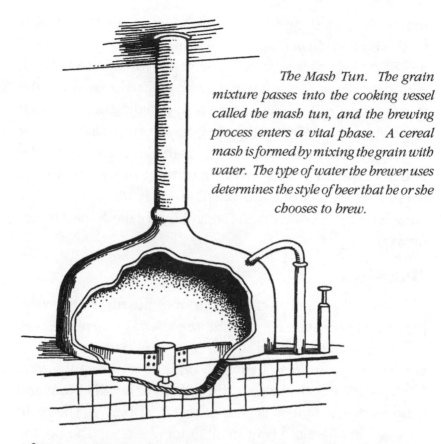

The Mash Tun. The grain mixture passes into the cooking vessel called the mash tun, and the brewing process enters a vital phase. A cereal mash is formed by mixing the grain with water. The type of water the brewer uses determines the style of beer that he or she chooses to brew.

of time to attain this reaction, and, during this delay, it is possible for tannins to soak out of the husk. For this reason, most brewers today choose the calcium method for controlling pH.

When the brewer is sure that the pH is set where he or she wants it, the grain and the water cereal mash mixture can then be pushed on to the next step in the process. Heat on the mixture is increased to a range where natural enzymes in the grain activate and then breakdown the grain's stored starches into fermentable sugars. In some systems, two vessels are used for heating, the second vessel being the *lauter tun*. If the single vessel is used to apply the heat, the process is called *infusion*. If two vessels are used, small amounts of mash are removed, heated, and then returned to the mash tun, in a method called *decoction.* The mashing procedure of holding the grain and water mixture in the vessel for a period of time allows the natural enzymes within the malt to break down the starches into sugars that can be fermented. The sugar-rich water is then strained through the bottom of the mash or lauter tun in a process called *lautering.* As the liquid drains off the grain, warm water is sprayed over the top to recover the maximum amount of sugar possible. This *sparging* process completes the recovery of the sugar liquid called sweet liquor or wort.

BREWING

The liquid that drains off the bottom of the tun is the sweet liquor and is next directed to the *brew kettle,* where the beer will begin to take its final shape. The heat in the brew kettle is raised until the *wort* begins to boil. It is during this vital boiling stage that the brewer, through his or her decisions and actions, dictates the outcome of the final brew. The techniques will affect the beer in all judging areas. The boiling stage of brewing involves many technical and chemical reactions, which are described for you here in detail.

During a process called *hot break,* the proteins coagulate and fall out of suspension, which is called *flocculate,* because of the vigorous agitation of boiling. The rolling action of the boil is what causes the proteins to bump into each other, clump together, and fall to the bottom of the brew kettle. Many commercial breweries install mechanical agitators in the brew kettles to aid the coagulation process. A benefit of hot break is that tannins, which have a negative charge, are attracted to proteins, which have a positive charge. The two join and fall out of suspension, reducing the possibility of haze in the final product.

Next, the brewer adds hops, which impart bitterness when added early in the boil, flavor when added in the middle of the boil, and aroma when added at the finish of the boil. Again, in this instance, the flavor, color and aroma of the beer are in the capable hands of the masterbrewer. It is believed that hops interfere with the hot break. For this reason, some brewers wait until after the hot break to make their first hop addition. *Isomerization* is the technical name for the process of extracting the hop bitterness. Since hop resins are not readily soluble with water at room temperatures, solubility is accomplished by boiling for 30–90 minutes, although 60 minutes is usually sufficient time. The high heat of the boil causes this chemical reaction called isomerization. Through this method, the resin is altered into a different form of the same chemical, with the new form being water soluble. The high heat and rolling boil contribute to high hop utilization. Lower utilization is often the result of low heat, short boils, and concentrated wort in the brew kettle.

Under the heat of brewing, sugars and amino acids can combine to form *melanoidins,* which darken the beer in a process often referred to as *caramelization.* (This caramelization can also be controlled by the intensity of the boil.) These melanoidins are also formed during the kilning process and give malt its dark color and malty flavor. Concentration can also affect this darkening in the brew kettle. A higher concentrated wort in a smaller brew kettle produces a beer of darker color. Therefore, to obtain a pale beer and high hop utilization, large brew kettles are preferred.

Hop oils and their aroma come from the *lupulin gland* of the hop. They are readily soluble in water, are very volatile, and will quickly boil off. To impart aroma, the brewmaster adds hops to the brew kettle at the very end of the boil. Then, the wort drains through fresh hops placed in a device called a *hop back* or *hop jack*. This strainer filters out the hops as the wort passes through. The wort is next sent to a *whirlpool*, where it is spun. The purpose of the spinning is to create the centrifugal force necessary to remove any remaining bits of hops or grain that could make the beer too harsh. The whirlpool also removes long molecules of protein that could give the beer a cloudy appearance or haze.

COOLING

The wort is transferred quickly from the brew kettle, through the hop back and whirlpool, and onto a *heat exchanger,* where it is cooled. Although there are many types of heat exchangers, in its simplest form it may be thought of as a coil of tubing. The wort flows through the inside of the tubing while the outside sits in a cool tub of water. This quick cooling is necessary to lower the temperature of the wort to a point where yeast can be safely added. Since yeast cannot grow or ferment in high heat, a temperature of about 70°F. is most desirable.

At this point, the brewer must measure the amount of sugars extracted from the beer. This is done with the use of a *hydrometer,* which measures the density of the liquid. Some wort is typically drawn off, and the hydrometer is placed in the sample. The more sugar that is present, the more dense the liquid is, and the higher the hydrometer will float in the solution. A reading is taken off the scale printed on the side of the hydrometer. This reading is called the *specific gravity,* and the higher the reading the more sugars there are available for fermentation. A typical wort gravity will read 1.05 for common beers. The homebrewer measures gravity using this same method. Many good homebrew shops, such as those listed in Appendix Three of this book, will stock hydrometers and all other materials needed for homebrewing.

FERMENTATION

Yeast is the most essential and least understood aspect of brewing and fermentation. Since the 1850s, this single-celled organism has been the focus of studies that secured fame for scientists such as van Leeuwenhoik, Pasteur, Lavoisier, and Guy-Lussac. Yet the mystery of its work still remains. Ferment comes from the Latin word for "boil," and anyone who looks at a glass container of fermenting beer and observes the turbulent action cannot help but marvel at the mystery of yeast and fermentation. There are various phases of the yeast lifecycle, which are described for you here in detail.

The lifecycle of yeast begins with *pitching,* the brewer's term for adding the yeast to the cooled wort. After passing through the heat exchanger, the cooled wort is directed to the *fermentation tank.* The brewer adds or pitches the yeast into the fermentation tank after it has been filled with the wort. This pitching must be done when the wort is at the proper temperature, which varies from 70°–80°F. Fermentation temperatures also vary depending upon the type of yeast used. For instance, the proper fermentation temperatures for ales are 55°–65°F., while for lagers the proper temperatures are 40°–55°F. Some fermentation tanks are shaped with a conical bottom so the flocculating yeast will occupy a small surface area on the bottom. This fermentation tank is the site of the real magic of brewing. It is here that the yeast changes the sugars into alcohol over a period of days or weeks, depending upon the style of the beer being brewed.

The first phase of this process is the *lag* phase. This is marked by the breaking of proteins into amino acids for nutrients and the building of food reserves in the yeast cell.

The ferment then passes into the *respiration* or *aerobic* phase, during which time the yeast absorbs oxygen and reduces pH. Once the yeast enters the respiration phase, the possibility of contamination decreases significantly, since the acidic and anaerobic environment is fairly hostile to most contaminants. Oxygen is used to synthesize complex fatty substances which are vital components of the yeast cell wall. As the phase progresses, all the oxygen is consumed and anaerobic respiration occurs. The yeast breaks down the glucose sugar and turns it into CO_2, H_2O, and pyruvic acid. Pyruvic acid is the precursor to alcohol. During the final stage of fermentation, the population of active yeast cells increases, as does the alcohol level.

There are other important events that occur during fermentation that are not part of the yeast lifecycle, but which can affect the final outcome of the beer. *Attenuation* is the term used to describe the reduction of wort gravity or sugar density by the yeast. Different strains of yeast will exhibit varying abilities to reduce all the fermentation in the wort. *Autolysis* can occur when too much yeast is pitched, or when the beer is allowed to sit on its yeast bed too long. In this environment, there are not enough nutrients to support the cell population, which leads to the digestion of the yeast by its own enzymes. Autolysis will impart a rubbery or yeasty flavor to the beer.

It is important to remember, while learning about fermentation, that yeast can not ferment all types of sugars. Some starch and dextrin non-fermentable sugars will remain after the brewing process. Some of these dextrins are desirable, however, because these sugars contribute body and mouth feel to beer. Yeast will ferment glucose (also known as dextrose), maltose, sucrose, and fructose. Glucose generally is responsible for giving beer its sweet, mellow flavor, while sucrose can impart cidery tones. Maltose is perhaps the most common of sugars found in wort, while fructose is commonly used only in fruit beers or meads, due to its fruity and honey flavor.

Fermentation tanks are a vital part of the brewing process, as you have just learned from the outline of the way in which wort is fermented. It is possible for brewers and breweries to use different types of fermentation equipment, in order to impart unique characteristics to their beers. A *Burton Union* system, for instance, is made up of linked casks and troughs. One of the motivations for using a Burton Union is its ability to produce large amounts of yeast for processing and sale. As the beer ferments, its turbulence forces it to travel up through a swan-necked tube and into a trough. As it settles in the trough, it drains back into the cask. The yeast naturally resident in these halls of Burton Union imparts a distinctive fruitiness to the ale. The Marston brewery in England is the

The Burton Union System is made up of linked casks and troughs. This system affords the brewer the unique opportunity to produce large quantities of yeast, due to the inherent trough design. Only one brewery in the world uses this system today.

only brewery using a Burton Union system today, and garners its unique Classic Pale Ale from that system. The *Yorkshire Stone Square* is another unique system. It uses fermentation vats in which each wall of the vessel is quarried as a single piece of stone. Samuel Smith's Brewery in England is the only working system of this kind operating today.

Lambic has come to be known as an unusual, fruity style of beer which utilizes unmalted wheat and hops which are aged up to three years. However, Lambic is most notably a method of fermentation that dates back centuries. Lambic beer is only made in the Senne region of Belgium which has its own unique strain of wild yeast. After brewing, the wort is placed in an open cooling vessel in a brewhouse where the roof slats are opened to allow wind-blown wild yeast to ferment spontaneously.

Stein fermenting is yet another unusual type of fermentation that utilizes rock boiling. According to legend, this method was introduced when brewing was done in wooden tanks which could not be heated by an outside flame. This style beer, today referred to as "rauchenfels," is brewed by heating large rocks and dumping them into the brew kettle where they give up their heat and boil the wort. In the process, some of the wort is caramelized onto the stone. This caramelized wort is later returned to the beer as the stones are placed in the lagering tanks. It is important to be aware of these unusual systems simply because of the unique flavors the special fermenting techniques impart to beer.

RACKING

As discussed earlier, the brewer takes measurements of gravity prior to pitching and again after active fermentation, using the hydrometer. Specific gravity of the beer is based upon the density of water, which equals 1.000. Alcohol has a density which is slightly lower than that of water. As the yeast ferments the wort sugars into alcohol, the specific gravity drops. The difference between the initial (original) specific gravity and the ending (final) reading of specific gravity is the amount of alcohol present in the solution. The formula used to determine the percent of alcohol present is computed by subtracting the final gravity from the original gravity. Then this number is multiplied by 105 to get the percent alcohol by weight. To determine the alcohol content by volume, the brewer must multiply alcohol by weight by 1.25.

When the brewer's measurements of final gravity remain the same for several days in a row, usually at a measurement at or close to 1.012, fermentation is complete and the racking phase is set to begin. During this phase, the brewer will move or *rack* the beer from a level just above where the yeast has settled into a new vessel, called the *conditioning tank*. The brewer then patiently waits for the beer to complete its aging process. The homebrewer takes the equivalent step of transferring the liquid to a secondary fermenter.

FINISHING

The next step in the brewing process is filtration, followed by carbonation, which is accomplished by one of two basic methods. The traditional manner is to *prime* the young beer with more fermentable sugars at racking. The method of priming relies upon the healthy condition of yeast cells that have remained in suspension in the beer. Even a beer that appears brilliant contains enough active yeast cells to ensure carbonation. Additional yeast may only be needed if there has been an extremely long lagering period during which it may be difficult to raise the yeast from dormancy.

The brewer has a choice of several raw materials for use during priming. Most homebrewers and small-scale brewers prime with corn sugar or malt extract. The disadvantage of corn sugar is the relatively large bubble size it produces in the head. It typically does not offer the fine head produced through the use of other methods. Malt extract is a preferred method of brewers today because of the fine head it produces and because of the reduced chance of off-flavors. In liquid form, the priming malt is called *gyle*. With the *krausening* method, newly fermenting wort takes the place of corn sugar or malt extract. The disadvantage to krausening is that the bottle-fermentation may deposit a ring of yeast and hop resins at the neck of the bottle. This can lead to the premature and incorrect conclusion that there is bottle infection.

Finally, artificial carbonation is common among large brewers and among homebrewers who keg their product. Injection of CO_2 is done by placing 25–30 pounds of pressure (psi) on the keg and shaking it vigorously for 5–10 minutes. An injection carbonator is also used by large brewers to inject CO_2 into the beer as it flows to the bottling machine. Following the finishing phase comes the bottling or kegging of the product, which leads to the most important phase — the tasting!!

CHAPTER 3

STYLES

These profiles are descriptions to be used as a benchmark in the evaluation of beers. In tasting and judging, you should compare the style being sampled with these outlines and the suggested commercial samples. The profiles include the term *SRM* which is the Standard Research Method. It is a method of ranking beer color in which the higher numbers indicate the darker beers. (See the SRM chart in this book.) The value of International Bittering Units *(IBU)* is hop bitterness. The lower the number, the less bitter the beer.

GERMAN ALES

Alt— A beer associated with the city of Duesseldorf, "alt" is the German word for old. The Alt style uses a top-fermenting ale yeast, but then is cold-aged. Alt is a medium-bodied beer; some wheat may be used in variations. The color is copper/amber at 10–19 SRM. It has high hops at

A large array of glass types, sizes, and thicknesses are used for sampling over 70 beer styles available today from large and small brewers alike.

28–40 IBU with some low to slight hint of fruity aroma from esters. *Gravity* = 1.040–1.050. *Commercial examples:* DAB Dark, Widmer, Zum Uerige.

Kolsch—Kolsch is one of only two beer styles which, like Bordeaux wines, is an appellation, meaning it may only be brewed in the area of Koln (Cologne), Germany. Kolsch is a blond Alt-style beer with a light to medium body. It is pale to dark straw in color at 3.5–5 SRM. Hops are medium to assertive at 20–30 IBU. *Gravity* = 1.040–1.045. *Commercial examples:* difficult to find in the United States; in Germany, Kuppers, Fruh, Sion, Gaffel, Muhlen, Gilden.

GERMAN MALTED WHEAT ALES

Weizen or Weissbier—From southern Germany, Weizen beer has a light to medium body and is usually pale to golden in color. Unlike most beers, some cloudiness is acceptable in this style since a mash of up to 60 percent wheat can add haze from protein. Color of 3–9 SRM. Light hops are part of the profile known for a clove-like nose with some slight banana aroma. Hops are low at 8–14 IBU. *Gravity* = 1.045–1.055. *Commercial examples:* Paulaner, Hofbrauhaus.

Berliner Weisse — This tart, refreshing, thirst-quenching beer is an appellation, since it can only be brewed in Berlin. Often it is called the champagne of beers. Up to 60 percent wheat malt is used and results in a characteristic large white head. The ale-type yeast contains up to 20 percent lactobacillus and produces a light body which is dry, tart, and almost sour with high effervescence and low fruity notes. The beer is often served mixed with raspberry or woodruff syrup to counter the acidic notes. The color is very light at 2–4 SRM. Hopping is low, with IBU at 3–8. *Gravity:* The low alcohol level of about 3 percent is the product of gravities of 1.028–1.032. *Commercial examples:* Berliner Kindl Weisse, Schultheiss Berliner Weisse.

Hefe-weizen — Overall the profile of this beer is similar to Weizen. This is a real ale style that is conditioned in the bottle or keg and will contain some yeast sediment. *Commercial examples:* Pschorr Weizen, Wurzburger.

Dunkel Weizen — Dunkel Weizen is a medium- to full-bodied beer with an emphasis of dark malt. Dunkel Weizen exhibits a darker deep copper color of 17–22 SRM. As with others in the Weizen category, it produces the characteristic clove-banana aromas. Hops are in the range of 10–15 IBU. *Gravity* = 1.045–1.055 but often is quite stronger. *Commercial example:* EKU.

Weizenbock — A medium- to full-bodied beer, it is made from 40–60 percent wheat, but the palate emphasis is on the malt. The color may range from deep copper to dark brown; 7–30 SRM. The hop flavor and aroma are very low at 10–15 IBU, but the clove and banana flavor and aroma are still evident. *Gravity:* as in all bocks, the gravity must be at least

1.066, and usually extends up to 1.080. *Commercial examples:* Erdinger Pinkantus and Shneider Aventinius.

BELGIAN UNMALTED WHEAT ALES

Wit or White — This beer has a medium body made from up to 50 percent unmalted wheat. It is stronger and maltier than its Berlin cousin (Weiss) but not as acidic. Wit is tangy and sharply refreshing with hints of orange, honey, and even muscat. The color is cloudy and very pale yellow, ranging from 2–4 SRM, and sports a very white head. Noble hops (Noble hops are those noted for their aromatics) flavor and aroma should be noticeable, 20–30 IBU. *Gravity* = 1.044–1.050. *Commercial examples:* Hoegaarden Witbier, Celis Wit.

Lambic — A classic Belgian style, it has a medium body with up to 40 percent unmalted wheat, and a strong cleanly sour acidic character. Produced by spontaneous fermentation of the wort, this beer is only produced in the Senne Valley, a region south and west of Brussels. Younger versions are cloudy and golden yellow color with pinkish/amber found in older samples at 6–15 SRM. Lambic has low carbonation and is fruity. In what is usually an unthinkable process, the hops are aged for up to three years with IBU of 11–22. *Gravities* = 1.047–1.054. *Commercial example:* Belle-Vue.

There are several specific variations of lambic. These all have the general lambic profile with some deviations: Fox is a young, golden yellow, very effervescent variation, usually blended with older lambics to make Gueuze. Gueuze is a blend of young and old lambic. After blending, it may be conditioned for an additional 6–9 months before it is released. This beer can be laid down for two and possibly as long as five years. A beer of golden to amber color, it becomes darker with age. SRM is 6–13. Gueuze is noticeably sharp, tart, and acidic but not bitter with IBU ranging 11–23. *Gravity* = 1.044–1.056.

Commercial example: St. Louis. Vieux, which literally means "old," are the aged, mature lambics. The color usually deepens with age.

Faro is a Lambic that has sugar and sometimes caramel added to produce a "sweet and sour" beer. So much alcohol is formed that it inhibits further fermentation and leaves behind residual sugars. A Faro will have moderate carbonation, with a fruity and complex flavor. The color is cloudy and golden yellow at 8–13 SRM. There are no noticeable hops at 11–22 IBU. *Gravity* = 1.047–1.054.

BELGIAN ALES

These more traditional styles of ale are related to the varieties found in the U.K. but use a greater variety of yeast strains than the original, and those different yeast strains produce a wider range of flavors. Belgian brewers sometimes use up to three different yeasts in primary, secondary, and bottle stages of the brewing process.

Pale—The pale ales of Belgium span a broad spectrum of characteristics. They share the general characteristics of the English pale ales, however, are of light amber to copper in color. These ales may include candy sugar or other aromatics. They are light to medium in body, with low malt aroma, and low carbonation. The hops are 25–35 IBU. *Gravity* = 1.048–1.070. *Commercial example:* De Konnick.

Trappist Ales—Only six breweries in the world, all located in active monasteries, may use the appellation "Trappist." They are the Westmalle, Orval, Rochefort, Westvleteren, and Chimay breweries in Belgium, and the Trappists of Schaapskooi in the Netherlands.

The Trappist ales are regarded as some of the finest ales in the world, and it is not uncommon to see them listed with designations such as *Grand Cru* in the same manner as fine wines. They are bottle-conditioned beers, and other Belgian brewers have labeled this as *Methode Champenoise*. The yeast strains and brewing techniques produce esters, which add a fruity character, as well as a spicy flavor with a slight sourness. The terms for Trappist classifications are not exact, but in general a single is the lowest gravity and is the monks' house or everyday beer. A double (*dubbel*) is stronger, and the triple (*tripple*) is extra potent; the latter two are used for holidays and religious celebrations. The ales are dark amber to brown for the singles and doubles, 10–25 SRM. The doubles are darker than the singles and are malty with a slightly nutty aroma. They have medium to full body. The triples are typically light to pale in color, and medium- to full-bodied with a light malt/hops aroma; Hops 20–40 IBU. *Single and double gravities* = 1.060–1.070; *triple gravity* = 1.070–1.095.

Saison—A Belgian top-fermented beer for summer drinking, it is often only 50 percent attenuated (fermented). The color may range from blond to amber, SRM 3.5–10. Saisons are bottle-conditioned with additional yeast added to the bottle. These were designed before the arrival of refrigeration as a laying-down beer for over the summer non-brewing period. The profile includes a dense head on a fairly well-carbonated beer with a palate of some tart, citric notes. The hopping rate is 20–30 IBU. They are usually dry-hopped as well, quite often with Belgian grown British varieties. *Gravity* = 1.050–1.080. *Commercial examples:* Saison Dupont, Saison Silly.

Belgian Red — This red beer is often referred to as the Burgundy of Belgium. A sour red beer of light to medium body, it contains up to twenty strains of yeast. The taste is surprisingly tart (*lactobacilli*) with a wide range of fruitiness. The red color, 10–18 SRM, comes, in part, from the use of Vienna malt, but also is derived from aging in the brewery's uncoated oak tuns. Hops are Kent Goldings and Brewers Gold, but this is not a hoppy beer. *Gravity* = 1.052–1.056.

Flanders Brown Ales — The color lends the name for this flavorful beer that runs from deep copper to brown at an SRM of 10–30. These ales are slightly sour and spicy with a fruity and estery palate. The yeast imparts a somewhat lactic character, and there may be some low diacetyl (butterscotch). There is no hop aroma and low to medium bitterness, 25–40 IBU. *Gravity* = 1.035–1.053. *Commercial example:* Liefmans Goudenband.

Belgian Strong Golden Ales — The names and references to the devil are often a trademark of these beers. Perhaps this is in direct correlation to the idea that the devil may pay if these are the subject of overindulgence. Typically, these beers are pale to golden in color, 3–5.5 SRM. The light color and deceiving body are the result of very pale malt. Top-fermented and cold-conditioned, hops are at 30 IBU. *Gravity* = 1.060–1.070. *Commercial examples:* Duvel, Lucifer, Teutenbier, Deuginiet.

Belgian Dark Strong Ales — There are many variations of this Belgian style which is characterized by full body and a deep burgundy to brown color, 25–35 SRM. Rich, creamy, and sweet, these ales are malty with low hops. The hops are 25–35 IBU. *Gravity* = 1.070–1.096. *Commercial examples:* Pawel Kwak, Bush, Gouden Carolus.

Biere de Garde — Typically made with several malts, this is a strong, top-fermenting, laying-down beer, quite commonly corked not capped. Bière de Garde is a dark amber colored brew at 25–40 SRM. It has a malty and fruity aroma and is hopped to a rate of approximately 25 IBU. *Gravity* = 1.060–1.075. *Commercial examples:* Trois Monts, Jenlain, La Choulette, Saint Leonard.

STYLE PROFILES OF BITTERS				
Type	**Body**	**IBU**	**SRM**	**Gravity**
Ordinary Bitter	light to medium	20–25	8–12 gold to amber	1.035–1.038
Special Bitter	medium (more malt)	25–30	12–14 amber to copper	1.039–1.042
Extra Special Bitter	full	30–35	12–14 copper	1.043–1.050
Commercial examples: Red Hook ESB, Youngs, Fullers, Hales, Pyramid				

PROFILES OF SCOTTISH ALES				
Type	**Body**	**IBU**	**SRM**	**Gravity**
Scottish Light (60-Shilling)	mildest	10–15	10–17 pale amber	1.030–1.035
Scottish Heavy (70-Shilling)	medium to full, malty and round	12–17	10–19 pale to dark amber	1.035–1.040
Scottish Export (80-Shilling)	full, drier, more bitter	15–20	10–19 pale to dark amber	1.040–1.050
Commercial examples: Belhaven, MacAndrews, McEwens				

PALE ALES

Bitter — This term comes from the days when English breweries used it to differentiate this type of ale from their milder version. Often, the taste and aroma is nearly identical to that of pale ales. Usually a draft (most English ales are consumed in pubs), it is traditionally cask-conditioned. Bitters have a copper-red color, 8–12 SRM. There are some esters, and it is possible to detect a trace of diacetyl. The styles vary along geographic lines, with the northern type being maltier, stronger, and less carbonated, while the southern type is more aggressively hopped and carbonated. Hops used in this style beer are Northern Brewer, Fuggles, Brewers Gold, and Chinook along with dry hopping of Goldings.

Scottish Ales—These are browner, more full-bodied ales, and are chewier than English ales. Scottish ales have a maltier aroma than English ales are known to possess. This type of ale is fermented at cooler temperatures than English ales and results in less fruity esters. Early in the history of the style, there was probably a smokey flavor from malt dried by burning peat. Their distinctive color and dryness is derived from roasted or black malts, and their underlying sweetness is derived from crystal. The "shilling" designation is believed to be from the old method of taxing by basing the tax rate on the gravity of the beer. The style is very full-bodied; the color is deep gold to deep amber/brown; SRM 10–19. Hopping rates are 10–20 IBU. Malt is the very evident flavor and aroma.

English Pale Ale—This is really a misnomer, since pale ale is not really pale, although it is lighter in color than porter. The colors range from light to pale amber with many as deep as copper. Typically, this category includes bitters as well. Pale ales are bottled, medium-bodied, with dry to low maltiness, hoppy and well-attenuated. They are fruity and estery and there can be some low diacetyl. Color is 6–12 SRM. The hops used in this style are traditionally Goldings, but can include Northern Brewers or Brewers Gold. Dry hopping is common in better examples, using Goldings, Cascade or Hallertauer, which are among the most expensive hops available to brewers today. IBU 20–40. *Gravity* = 1.044–1.056. *Commercial examples:* Worthington White Shield, Samuel Smith's, Bass, Royal Oak, Whitbread Pale Ale.

American Pale Ale — The popularity of pale ale comes from the microbrewery and pub renaissance in America which has escalated in the last five years. In comparison to its English counterpart, this American pale ale is slightly less malty, in the range of low to medium. It is fruity and estery with some crystal malt providing a bit of residual sweetness. Color is pale straw to amber; 4–11 SRM. A distinction of the American version is the high hopping of American varieties: Chinook, Cluster, Eroica, and Perle, with Cascade and Willamette added for aroma. IBU are 20–40. Dry hopping is appropriate. *Gravity* = 1.045–1.056. *Commercial examples:* Sierra Nevada Pale Ale, Hopland Red Tail Ale, Red Hook Ale. Stock ale is generally in the pale ale style, and is a slightly stronger version meant for longer storage. It is not necessarily a separate category, however.

India Pale Ale — This classic style was born of necessity when English brewers were making a beer for export to the troops in Colonial India. Transporting these beers required a long sea voyage down the coast of Africa, around the Cape and through several drastic temperature changes. Thus, a high gravity beer was developed so it could finish maturing at sea. High hops were added for preservation. An IPA should have a medium body with evident alcohol. It can have fruity or estery notes, yet the diacetyl should be low. The color is pale amber/copper; SRM 8–18. An identifying characteristic is the high-hop bitterness, flavor, and aroma. Goldings, Galena, or Brewers Gold are added for bitterness. Aroma is from Fuggles, Cascade, or Tettnang; IBU 40–60. Goldings or Cascade are used to dry hop. *Gravity* = 1.050–1.064. *Commer-*

cial examples: Anchor Liberty Ale, Sierra Nevada Celebration Ale, Young's Special London Ale, Ballantine's Old India Pale Ale.

BROWN ALES

Mild — Originating in coal mining areas of England and Wales, this was a low-alcohol beer designed for generous consumption by manual laborers. The style is sweeter and paler than porter, and the body is as malty as is possible in a low gravity beer. The color is deep copper to dark brown, and is derived from a mixture of malts; SRM 17–34. Golding, Fuggle, and Bullion hops are used, but there is very little hop aroma; IBU 12–25. *Gravity* = 1.032–1.036. *Commercial example:* Grant's Celtic Ale.

English Brown — The English browns are sweeter and more full-bodied than the English milds; in fact they are the bottled equivalent of mild ale. In general, these brews are medium-bodied. From this distinction, the style splits along geographic lines. Southern brown ales are darker, are sweet, and are made from low gravities. The southern England versions have a medium body and dark brown color, SRM 15–22. Some fruitiness and esters are present. English hops such as Goldings and Fuggles are used with low flavor and aroma at rates of 15–25 IBU. *Gravity* = 1.040–1.050. *Commercial example:* Watney's Mann's Brown Ale. Northern varieties, though still medium-bodied, are less sweet, with a pale copper color, 12–18 SRM. Some esters and fruitiness are present, and the hops are similar to the southern, 15–25 IBU. *Gravity* = 1.040–1.050. The northern browns have been described as close cousins to a bitter. *Commercial examples:* Samuel Smith's Old Brewery Strong Brown Ale, Newcastle Brown.

American Brown — American versions of brown ale tend to be drier with higher hops than their English counterparts.

Some maltiness is present in a medium body. Color is 15–22 SRM. Hops are American varieties, such as Galena and Chinook, with Eroica used in bittering and Cascade used for aroma. The hops are assertive at 25–60 IBU. *Gravity* = 1.040–1.055. *Commercial examples:* Cooper Smith's Dunraven Ale, Hart's Pacific Crest Ale.

PORTER

This style emerged from the London area in the early 1700s. It has a somewhat dry, malty character and is dark with a red hue. More specifics are hard to come by, and therefore, many beer experts agree that historically, porter is one of the most elusive beer styles in existence. Brewing of this style began as an early marketing response to the consumer ordering several different beers mixed together in a concoction called "entire." The ale brewed to replicate this effect came to be known as porter. One story attributes the current name to London produce market porters who favored the style. There are two widely recognized types of porters, robust and brown.

Robust Porter — This variety presents a medium to full body in a balanced beer that has a noticeably dry, malty flavor. Chocolate and black malts add a sharp bitterness, but do so without roasted or charcoal notes. The color is deep with red hues, but is not opaque like stout; SRM 30+. Hops such as Northern Brewer, Perle, and Chinook are favored for this brew. Cascade used at the finish in dry hopping can produce an appropriate low hop aroma; IBU 25–40. *Gravity:* Originally, the gravity was thought to be about 1.070, but today's versions are in the range of 1.045–1.058. *Commercial examples:* Anchor Porter, Sierra Nevada Porter, Black Hook Porter.

Brown Porter — The brown porter style is a bit lighter

variety than the robust, with light to medium body. Typically, the malt is well-balanced with the hops. Color is deep with reddish tones; SRM 20–35. Bittering hops used in this style include Northern Brewer, Chinook, and Brewers Gold. Low to medium aroma hops utilized include Hallertauer and Cascade used at the finish. IBU 20–30. *Gravity* = 1.040–1.050. *Commercial examples:* Samuel Smith's Taddy Porter, Young's London Porter.

STOUT

This style is often referred to as "Porter's Big Brother" and was originally called stout-porter, before shortening its name to stout. As in other styles, there is some variety in the stout family. In general, it is dark and opaque but, as with porter, there are variations which include: dry stout, foreign stout, sweet stout, oatmeal stout, and imperial stout.

Dry Stout—Sometimes called Irish Stout, this is the direct descendent of porter. Low- to medium-bodied, the distinguishing feature is the use of roasted barley to produce a slightly roasted (coffee-like) trait. It starts with a taste of malt and caramel and ends with a dry-roasted, bitter taste. There may be low to medium diacetyl. Color is 40+ SRM. There is just enough English variety hop flavor present to offset the malt. Thus, there is no noticeable hop flavor or aroma. IBU are 30–40. *Gravity* = 1.038–1.042. *Commercial examples:* Guinness, Sierra Nevada.

Foreign Stout—This is a stronger version of dry with the additional malt offset by hopping up to 60 IBU for balance. *Gravity* = 1.050–1.070. *Commercial example:* Guinness Extra Stout.

Sweet Stout—This style was commonly called Milk Stout, although the name milk is no longer allowed to be used in conjunction with a beer style within England. Differentiated by lower gravity than dry and possessing a unique chocolate-caramel malt flavor, the roasted trait of other stouts is mini-mized in milk stout. The flavor is derived from the use of chocolate malt and milk sugar (lactose). The characteristics include a medium to full body with the typical opaque color; SRM 40+. There may be low diacetyl detected. Hops are used in the bittering to balance the inherent sweetness, but the bitterness is low and there is no hop flavor or aroma. IBU are 15–25. *Gravity* = 1.038–1.045. *Commercial example:* Mackenson.

Oatmeal Stout—This beer is a variation of the sweet stout but has oatmeal added to increase the fullness of body and flavor. The result of this mixture is often described by beer enthusiasts as a silkiness not found in other beers. *Commercial example:* Samuel Smith's Oatmeal Stout.

Imperial Stout — The name Imperial comes from an ancient contract between an English brewery and the Russian court which stipulated that the brewery would provide stout to the Court. High gravity and hops are used to prepare these for export, much as was done with India Pale Ale. Full-bodied, it is dark copper to black with color at 20+ SRM. As you might imagine, the high gravity leads to notable esters and fruitiness and the preserving hops impart a high level of hop bitterness, aroma, and flavor. IBU 50–80+. *Gravity* = 1.075–1.095+. *Commercial example:* Samuel Smith's Imperial Stout.

STRONG ALE

English Old Ale — Also called Strong Ale, this beer is generally served on draft, and it is often hard to tell the difference between an old ale style beer and a barley wine (see Barley Wine later in this section). Both names are used to describe strong beers, however, in most cases, the barley wine will prove to be a bit stronger. These are laying-down beers, which are a bit syrupy when young, but improve with up to five years of aging. English old ales are very full-bodied, with a nutty malt sweetness, and are very estery. Color is usually on the pale end, with a range of 10–16 SRM. Hopping is assertive with rates at 30–60 IBU, but hop aroma is low from the aging process. Well-attenuated, the *Gravity* = 1.060–1.075+. *Commercial examples:* Theakston's Old Peculiar and Thomas Hardy's, which is often classified a barley wine.

Scottish Ale — These come with the familiar shilling designation we examined earlier in the pale ale category. These strong ale shilling designations are even higher at 90, 100, 110, and even 120 shilling. The fermentation is roused so the yeast will stay in suspension and attenuate the beer. This is a full-bodied beer with color that is deep copper to brown, SRM 10–45. There can be medium diacetyl present. These beers are much less hopped than English versions, and therefore are maltier, at 25–35 IBU. *Gravity* = 1.072–1.085. *Commercial examples:* MacAndrew's Scotch Ale, McEwan's Scotch Ale, Traquir House.

Barley Wine — Some beer experts point out that this is a rather new name for a style that is actually "strong" or "old" ale. The flavor profile is very near to strong ale, full-bodied, with the yeast roused to assure thorough attenuation and evident alcohol. These beers are characterized by their assertive hops and low aroma, both of which may diminish during aging. The aroma includes esters, and there can be some low to medium diacetyl. If there is a distinction to be made between barley wines and strong ales, it is in the darker color of barley wines. Also, English brewers tend to call the highest gravity brews barley wines, while Americans tend to refer to the same concoction as strong ales. Another distinguishing characteristic is that old ales are usually on draft, while barley wines are more commonly bottled. The barley wine profile is: color deep gold to brown, 14–40 SRM; IBU at 50–100; *Gravity* = 1.090–1.120. *Commercial examples:* Anchor Old Foghorn Barley Wine, Sierra Nevada Big Foot Barley Wine, and, once again, Thomas Hardy Ale.

Lagers

Unlike ales, the beers in this group are bottom-fermented at lower temperatures. Early brewers who stored their beer in ice caves for summer consumption found that the long, cold fermentation resulted in clear and bright beers. This was caused, in part, by the inability of bacteria to exist in the cold. In addition, the long, cold aging assisted in dropping any haze out of suspension. The beer styles that follow are all classified under the general heading of lagers. Unless noted, esters and diacetyl are inappropriate in these lager beers.

American Diet/Lite— A far-removed cousin of the Czech lagers, it might be said this diet or light beer is low in everything. One joke likens light beer to canoe beer — both are pretty close to water. Low in body, light beer also has low or no malt taste and is very effervescent. Color is very pale; SRM 2–4. Hop bitterness from Clusters is below the threshold of taste and no flavor or aroma is detected; 8–15 IBU. *Gravity* = 1.024–1.040. *Commercial examples:* Miller Lite, Coors Light, Bud Light, Stroh's Light.

American Standard — Light in body, this style has low malt aroma and flavor. Large amounts of adjuncts, such as corn and rice, are used to lighten the body. Color is very pale; 2–3.5 SRM. Hop bitterness is barely noticeable with very low flavor and aroma; 5–17 IBU. *Gravity* = 1.040–1.046. *Commercial examples:* Budweiser, Coors, Stroh's.

American Premium — The profile for this style is very similar to that of the American standard style, except that there are usually fewer adjuncts in premium beers (25–30 percent), and rice is often substituted for corn. The body is light, with low malt flavor and aroma. Color is 2–4 SRM. Bitterness is low to medium from American varieties of Clusters, Cascade, and Willamette, but generally the hops are barely detectable. IBU range from 13–18. *Gravity* = 1.046–1.050. *Commercial examples:* Michelob, Henry Weinhard's Private Reserve, Coors Herman Joseph's.

American Dry — This is truly an engineered beer. The style did not originate in the United States, but, as with many new fads, it is borrowed from abroad, in this case from Japan's number one beer, Asahi. The beer uses a genetically-designed yeast to break down normally unfermentable sugars into a fermentable form. It may be thought of as a malt liquor of lower alcohol, 4–5 percent alcohol. There is very low body and malt, and almost no malt aroma. The most distinguishing marks to this style are its high effervescence, clear color, and lack of aftertaste. Color is 2–4 SRM. Hopping is at low rates of 15–23 IBU. *Gravity* = 1.040–1.050. *Commercial examples:* Michelob Dry, Asahi Dry.

American Dark — With the exception of color, these beers are very similar to American standard beers. The major difference is the inclusion of some dark malts, though the color can also be artificially derived from the addition of caramel syrup. Color 15–20 SRM; hops 14–20 IBU. *Gravity* = 1.040–1.050. *Commercial examples:* Henry Weinhard's Special Dark Reserve, Michelob Dark.

American Bock — Less assertive than European Bocks, this American style originated in Wisconsin and spread throughout the U.S. market. Bocks are almost identical to American dark beers, with just a bit darker color; SRM 4.5–12. American hops are added at 18–25 IBU. *Gravity* = 1.045–1.052. *Commercial examples:* Augsburger, Shiner. *Note:* For more on traditional Bocks, see the section on Continental Lagers.

American Malt Liquor— This is a pale lager beer roughly similar to other American lagers but higher in alcohol. The first attempts at producing a malt liquor were made through the use of *Aspergillus oryazae* bacteria to convert the unfermentables to fermentable sugars, with a corresponding increase in alcohol. Since then an engineered yeast has been introduced which simplifies the process. These beers are made to intentionally achieve very high level alcohol in the range of 5 percent up to 8 percent. The name "malt liquor" is a designation based on the fact that these brews quite often exceed the legal alcohol level defined for lagers and other beers. The anti-alcohol groups in the U.S. have also recently attacked the producers of this style beer for the very fact that these beers are so high in alcohol content. Very pale, the color is 1–3 SRM. Hopping is light at 5–14 IBU. *Gravity* = 1.048–1.064. *Commercial examples:* Molson Brador, Colt 45.

CLASSIC PILSNERS

Bohemian Pilsner— This is the style that should spring to the mind of beer lovers when pilsner is mentioned. This beer originally debuted in Plzen, Czechoslovakia, and quickly gained popularity in other brewing countries. Light- to medium-bodied, the beer benefits from extremely soft water. Pilsners characteristically have noticeable hop aroma and flavor. Esters are not appropriate in pilsners, but, in some of the classic renditions, such as Pilsner Urquell, which translates to "original source," low diacetyl adds a complexity. To beer drinkers, the bright, pale gold color is an immediately appealing characteristic. Color 2.5–4 SRM. Hops include noble varieties of Hallertauer and Tettnang, and the aroma is well defined by a finish of Saaz; IBU 25–45. *Gravity* = 1.045–1.056. *Commercial examples:* Pilsner Urquell, Budvar.

German Pilsner — The German version of this style is

simpler, cleaner, and from a lower extract than the original Czechoslovakian beer. The distinctive characteristic is the flowery hop bouquet and its dry finish from a more thorough fermentation. Color is 2.5–4 SRM. Hops are Splat, Tettnang, and Bavarian Northern Brewer with a Saaz finish; 30–40 IBU. *Gravity* = 1.044–1.048. *Commercial examples:* Warsteiner, Becks, Aass Pilsner, Pinkus Ur-Pils.

DORTMUNDER

Commonly called *Export,* this style fits into a class which is more attenuated and thus stronger than pilsners. It is, however, a bit less hoppy. The water in Dortmund is quite hard, and this, combined with a special malting process which results in increased enzyme power, contributes to the final unique taste of Dortmunder. Medium-bodied and sweeter than Pilsner, it has a pale to golden color of 4–6 SRM. The hops are Hallertauer, Tettnang, and Saaz, at 18–25 IBU. There are **no** traces of diacetyl or esters. *Gravity* = 1.050–1.056. *Commercial examples:* Dortmunder Union, Kronen, DAB, Saratoga.

VIENNA

Originated in 1841, this style beer is credited to the famous Austrian brewer, Anton Dreher. The style enjoyed a great following in Mexico and the southwest United States, but fell from favor elsewhere. This distinctive style owes much of its character to the method of malting. Malt provides the dominant toasty flavor, aroma, and unique color. This beer is of medium body with a reddish-amber color, 8–12 SRM. Very mild hops put the emphasis on the malt; aroma-type hops are used with IBU of 22–28. *Gravity* = 1.046–1.052. *Commercial examples:* Dos Equis Amber, Portland Lager, Ambier Genuine Vienna Style, Newman's Albany Amber.

Marzen or Oktoberfest—This style is credited to Munich's famous brewer Gabriel Sedelmayer, and the name originates from the days before refrigeration when March was the last brewing month. It was designed as a popular beer to be laid down in caves over the summer. Any of the beer that remained at the end of September was dispatched with ceremony. The ceremony celebrating the end of summer is the event that brought about the other sobriquet for this style. The name "Oktoberfest" came from the marriage of Bavarian heir Prince Ludwig to Princess Theresa in 1810. All the subjects were invited to join in the celebration. It was reportedly such a rollicking good time that the merrymaking still continues each year as a memorial sixteen-day party, which begins in late September. The style is an adaptation of Vienna that was found to better suit the Munich water. The body is medium, with medium to strong alcohol, malty aroma, and color of 7–14 SRM. IBU 22–28. *Gravity* = 1.052–1.065. *Commercial examples:* Gosser, Spaten Munich Ur-Marzen Oktoberfest, Paulaner Oktoberfest, Ayinger Fest Marzen, Harpoon Oktoberfest, Samuel Adams Octoberfest.

MUNICH

Helles — The name "helles" means pale, and this is the lighter (colored) version of Munich style beer which first appeared in the late 1920s. Before that time the style was referred to as a dark-colored "dunkel." Malty sweetness, often described as almost a caramel, is the mark of this beer. Part of the malty flavor comes from the unique Munich style of malting which involves "curing" the malt at temperatures of 212° to 225°F. For as much as pilsners are hoppy, Munich beers are malty. The body is a bit heavier than a Bohemian pils, but the alcohol is moderate. A deep golden color is at an SRM of 3–5. Hops are mild, from aromatic varieties, at 20–30

IBU.   *Gravity* = 1.045–1.055.   *Commercial examples:* Altenmunster, Ayinger Jahrhundert.

Munich Dunkel— This is the old style of Munich which predates helles. In German, "dunkel" means dark, and thus this lager is characterized by a dark brown color with a clean toasted, chocolate or caramel sweetness in aroma and flavor. It is more malty than hoppy, with low to moderate alcohol and medium body. Color ranges from dark amber to dark brown; SRM 14–23. Hop bitterness is medium to low from aroma-type hops such as Hallertauer, at 20–30 IBU. *Gravity* = 1.050–1.058.   *Commercial examples:* Paulaner, Konig Ludwig Dunkel, Frankenmuth Bavarian Dark, Ayinger Alt–Bayrisches Dunkel.

Schwarzbier—Although not strictly a Munich, Schwarzbier is an off-shoot of the Munich style. The name literally means "black beer," and it is still popular in the area around Kulmbach, Germany. The profile includes a medium body with malty aroma and low sweetness. The style may also have evidence of roasty malt which will impart some bitterness. Color is dark brown to black at 25–30 SRM. IBU 20–30. *Gravity* = 1.044–1.052.   *Commercial example:* Kulmbacher Monchshof Schwarzes Pils. This style is hard to find in the United States since it is still usually confined to Germany.

Rauchbier — Again, although not strictly a Munich, rauchbier is an off-shoot of the Munich beers. The translation of rauchbier is "smoke beer" which is popular in the region of Bamberg, Germany. In this brew, the barley gets a smokey flavor from kilning over a fire of beechwood. The basic formulation is similar to Oktoberfest, but the profile is noted by its assertive smokey aroma and flavor. The beer presents a full body and a generally sweet, malty taste beneath the smoke. The color is dark amber to dark brown at 10–20 SRM. Hop bitterness and aroma is low to medium at 20–30 IBU.

Gravity = 1.048–1.052.   *Commercial examples:* Kaiserdom Rauchbier, Maisel's Rauchbier, Schlenkria Rauchbier. (*Note:* the style also includes Rauchenfels which can be classified under both rauchbier and stein beer. See pages 22-23 for more unusual systems.)

BOCK

This style is credited to and named for Einbeck, Germany, with the name shortened to beck, which, with a Bavarian accent, became bock. The German translation is "goat" which accounts for the symbol of a billy goat used so freely on bock beers. The style has nothing to do with the common myth that this beer is obtained once a year when brewers clean out brewery tanks and bottle what is on the bottom. Rather, it is the water and malt that give this style some special characteristics. The bock beer is full-bodied with a prevalent malty sweetness that can include some chocolate undertones. It is traditionally dark and uses just enough hops to balance the malt. There is no fruitiness or esters but there may be low to medium diacetyl. The color is dark amber to dark brown; SRM 20–30. Hops are Hallertauer with balanced bitterness at 20–30 IBU, with no hop aroma. *Gravity:* By German law, bocks must be of at least 1.066 gravity, so the gravity range is 1.066–1.074.   *Commercial examples:* Einbeck Ur-bock, Hofbrauhaus Maibock.

Helles Bock — In general, these bocks possess the same characteristics of traditional bock except for the chocolate undertaste and helles' lighter color. Full-bodied, it has a predominantly malty taste. Color is gold to light amber; 4.5–6 SRM. Hops just balance the bitterness with no aroma; 20–35 IBU. *Gravity* = 1.066–1.068. *Commercial examples:* Ayinger Mai Bock, Pschorr Marzenbock, Sierra Nevada Pale Bock.

Dopplebock— This is a stronger version of bock which must have a gravity of at least 1.074. The original doppelbock was brewed by monks of St. Francis Paula, which later became the Paulaner Brewery. The beer was made as a "liquid bread" for consumption at Lent by the monks. The Paulaner doppelbock was named "Salvator" in homage to the Savior and is generally released near Easter. Other doppelbocks continue this tradition by ending their names in "ator." They are typically very full-bodied with intense malty sweetness and aroma. There is some similarity to the flavor of barley wine with some esters and diacetyl detectable. Color is dark amber to dark brown at 18–35 SRM. Hops just balance the malt at 17–27 IBU. *Gravity* = 1.074+. *Commercial examples:* Paulaner Salvator, Ayinger Celebrator, Spaten Optimator.

Eisbock—The strongest type of bock, its name comes from the German word for ice, which describes the production. First, a regular doppelbock is made, then the beer is lowered to cold temperatures of about 32°F. At this level, water will freeze, but alcohol will not. The ice from the frozen water is removed, leaving behind a beer with a higher concentrated amount of alcohol. The beer is very full-bodied with increased sweetness and warmth. Color is amber to dark brown; SRM 10–40. Though the numbers for hops are high (remember, a greater proportion of hops are needed in higher gravity worts because of lower hop utilization at high gravity) the detectable bitterness is low with rates of 26–33 IBU. *Gravity* = 1.092–1.116. *Commercial examples:* Kulminator, EKU "28," Kulmbacher Eisbock Bayrisch G'frorns.

HYBRID STYLES

California Common Beer—This style is also known as steam beer, a trademark of the Anchor Brewing Co. in California, one of the pioneers of the U.S. regional brewing movement. The name "steam" may have referred to the wildness of the beer, or the pressure in the casks. The brew process for this style consists of lager yeast, higher ale range temperatures, followed by fermentation in a large, shallow, pan-shaped vessel, followed by the warm conditioning process. The style was popular in the time of the gold rush and was widely produced throughout the Northwest. The style has since enjoyed a resurgence due to the popularity of so-called specialty beers in the U.S. This beer has been likened to an India Pale Ale (IPA) in taste with a medium body and a hint of caramel. The color is light amber to copper at 8–17 SRM. Hops are medium to high in bitterness and flavor, and medium in aroma at 35–45 IBU. *Gravity* = 1.044–1.055. *Commercial examples:* Anchor Steam, New England Amber.

Cream Ale—Originally called "lively ale" or "sparkling lager ale," this was originally produced as an American attempt to capture the popularity of the new lager styles of the late 1800s in Europe. Another account suggests cream ales were a blend of ale and lager. In this variation of using lager yeast, a warm ferment is followed by cold lagering. The profile includes light to medium body with high effervescence. The color is pale at 2–4 SRM. Some low esters may be detectable. Hop bitterness is low to medium, with low hop aroma; 10–22 IBU. *Gravity* = 1.044–1.055. *Commercial examples:* Genesee Cream Ale, Little Kings Cream Ale, Molson Golden Ale, Weinhard's Light American Ale.

OTHER BEER STYLES

Those listed in this section are less common varieties of beer, however they are included because of the frequency with which they appear in homebrew competitions.

Specialty beers are a grouping of beers that do not fit the other descriptions. This does not mean that any old combination of ingredients are used, but rather that the purposeful inclusion of additives (other than fruit) combine to impart unique characteristics. Some of these additives are maple syrup, sorghum, honey, chocolate, and pumpkin. Commercial examples are hard to locate but there are the occasional offerings, such as Buffalo Bill's Pumpkin Ale. Other standard styles of beer can have smoke added to enhance the flavor profile. Smoked types must have the major style characteristics readily recognized; the smoke should not be so powerful as to eliminate the base beer. Some styles, such as pilsners, do not readily lend themselves to smoke flavor, but a smoked porter can be most satisfying. Thus, the production of these relies upon the common sense and experience of the brewer. *Commercial examples:* Vermont Pub and Brewery Smoked Porter and the Otter Creek Brewery Smoked Porter.

Fruit beers or lambics are made with fruits, with cherries and raspberries being the most popular additives. The fruit flavor and aroma should be noticeable with slightly under-hopped versions of the parent style as the base. Other common fruits include, but are not limited to, lemons, oranges, blueberries, boysenberries, and loganberries. *Commercial examples:* Difficult to find nationally but are likely to be available in very localized areas, such as your local microbrewery or brewpub.

Herbed beers are prepared with a variety of herbs and spices including marjoram, cinnamon, garlic, peppers, spruce, juniper, cloves, anise, nutmeg, coriander, caraway, ginger, etc. They are generally made at a gravity range of 1.040–1.050; otherwise the alcohol level and aroma could mask the subtleties of the herbs and spice. *Commercial examples:* Buffalo Bill's Pumpkin Ale, Harpoon Winterfest.

Although it seems inappropriate, sake should be considered a beer style. Even though it is also called a rice wine, don't forget that some beers are called barley wines. It is also considered a beer because of the common use of rice as an adjunct in commercial breweries. Sake comes in several different sub-categories. All of these have the common traits of 12–20 percent alcohol and a clear to very pale color. Traditional sake is semi-dry to dry with no carbonation. Sparkling sake is re-primed in the bottle with rice syrup and yeast and again is very light colored. Other forms of sake may contain some amounts of other grains, but rice is the most prevalent base.

Ciders are also beverages that are grouped with "Other Styles" of beers. Cider comes from apple juice in a variety of styles and is usually fermented by wine yeast. There are four types of ciders known to us today. Still cider has a light body and apple flavor. Under 7 percent alcohol, it can be dry to sweet and is a clear, pale yellow color. Sparkling cider has many still traits with the addition of effervescence. Though sparkling, there should be no head or foam. Sparkling cider may be dry to sweet and light to medium in body. The color is clear pale yellow. New England-style cider has a strong apple aroma and a higher level of alcohol, at 8–14 percent. These ciders can be still or naturally sparkling. The New England style is medium-to-full-bodied with some tannins, but no "hot" alcohol taste. The color is pale to medium yellow. Adjuncts may include sugars, molasses, and/or raisins. Specialty cider is at least 75 percent apple juice, with the remainder made from a variety of adjuncts. The alcohol content must be below 14 percent, but any type of yeast can be used in the production. *Commercial examples:* Most prevalent at cider mills in regional pockets across the country.

Mead beers may also claim title as one of the oldest of alcoholic beverages. The origins of mead date back to 2,000 BC in Babylonian records. Mead beer was believed to increase fertility, and, in the Middle Ages was served to newlyweds throughout their first month of marriage. There is also a tale of a hollow tree that contained a bee hive. Speculation is that rain flooded the cavity and wild yeast took care of the rest. In fact there are reports of aborigine tribes tapping just such trees. Imagine those commercials if mead were as popular as American beer! Meads are produced from honey, yeast, water, and in subcategories, by the addition of herbs and fruits. The standard profile includes a color of very pale to deep yellow. Generally the lighter color honey is used in dry types while darker honey is used for sweet styles. The original gravities are quite high at 1.095–1.150; the final gravity determines how the mead is classified: dry at 0.996–1.009, medium at 1.010–1.019, and sweet from 1.020–1.050.

Traditional mead can be either sparkling or still. Still is dry, medium, or sweet to very sweet with a light to full body. Honey is the predominate flavor and aroma. There may be some low to fruity acidity, but there are no harsh flavors. Sparkling mead can be of dry to medium sweetness. There is honey character in the flavor and aroma. Body is light to medium.

There are also flavored meads. These types may be either still or effervescent. Still types may be light- to full-bodied, while the sparkling examples are light- to medium-bodied. The color and aroma should reflect the ingredients used. The names of these varieties and their ingredients are: Melomel — from fruits other than apples or grapes; Cyser — flavored from the use of apples; Pyment — produced with the additions of grapes; Hippocras — a variation of Pyment that includes spices; Methegiln — ingredients are honey, herbs, and spices; Braggot or Bracket — includes the use of malted barley.

Although the varieties such as sake, cider, and mead beers are not commonly seen, you may find one or more of these varieties cropping up at a show, a tasting, or on a Beer Judge Certification Program (BJCP) exam. As stated earlier, you may not love each and every style of beer, but the true beer enthusiast should certainly have a broad background which covers all styles.

BEERSTYLES

STYLE	ORIGINAL GRAVITY	BODY	COLOR
Lagers			
AMERICAN LAGERS	1.040–1.050	L	very pale SRM 2–4
DORTMUNDER (Export)	1.050–1.056	M	pale to gold SRM 4–6
MUNICH HELLES	1.045–1.055	M	deep golden SRM 3–5
CLASSIC PILSNERS Bohemian Pilsner	1.045–1.056	L–M	bright pale to gold SRM 2.5–4
German Pilsner	1.044–1.048	L–M	pale to gold SRM 2.5–4
VIENNA Vienna	1.046–1.052	M	reddish amber SRM 8–12
Marzen/Oktoberfest	1.052–1.065	M	amber SRM 7–14
BAVARIAN DARK Munich Dunkel	1.050–1.058	M	dark amber to darkbrown SRM 14–23
Schwarzbier	1.044–1.052	M	dark brown to black SRM 25–30
BOCK Bock	1.066–1.074	F	dark amber to dark brown SRM 20–30
Helles Bock	1.066–1.068	F	gold to amber SRM 4.5–6
Doppelbock	1.074 minimum	F	amber to dark brown SRM 18–35

IBU	CHARACTERISTICS	EXAMPLES
5–20	hops balanced in light body; little malt or hops detected	Bud, Miller, Coors, Stroh's, Pabst
18–25	more attenuated; sweeter; less hoppy than pils	Dortmunder Union, Kronen, DAB
20–30	malty sweet, almost caramel; as pils are hoppy; Munich beers are malty	Altenmunster
25–45	hoppy nose and flavor; no diacetyl; no esters	Pilsner Urquell, Budvar
30–40	simpler, cleaner; lower hops than bohemian	Warsteiner Aass pils
22–28	malty; slightly toasty; emphasis on the malt	Dos Equis, Portland Lager
22–28	malty; medium to strong alcohol; brewed in March	Paulaner, Ayiner, Spaten
20–30	toasted chocolate or caramel sweetness	Paulaner, Konig Ludwig
20–30	malty aroma; low sweetness	Kulmbacher
20–30	malty sweetness with some chocolate undertones; no hop aroma; low to medium diacetyl	Hofbrauhaus
20–35	malty without the chocolate tones	Ayinger, Pschorr, Sierra Nevada
17–27	intense malty sweetness; "ator" in honor of the savior	Salvator, Celebrator

STYLE	ORIGINAL GRAVITY	BODY	COLOR
Eisbock	1.092–1.116	F	amber to dark brown SRM 10–40
Hybrid Beers: Lagers and Ales			
ALT German Alt	1.040–1.050	M	copper to amber SRM 10–19
Kolsch	1.040–1.045	L–M	pale to dark straw SRM 3.5–5
RAUCHBIER	1.048–1.052	M	amber to brown SRM 10–20
WHEAT BEERS Weizen	1.045–1.055	L–M	straw SRM 3-9
Hefe-Weizen	1.045–1.055	L–M	straw SRM 3–9
Berliner Weisse	1.028–1.032	L	pale SRM 2–4
Dunkel Weizen	1.045–1.055	M–F	deep copper SRM 17–22
Weizenbock	1.066–1.080	M–F	deep copper to brown SRM 7–30
CREAM ALE	1.044–1.055	L–M	pale SRM 2–4
CALIFORNIA COMMON	1.044–1.055	M	light amber to copper SRM 8–17

IBU	CHARACTERISTICS	EXAMPLES
26–33	alcohol warmth; malt sweetness; alcohol boosted by freezing out water	EKU "28"
28–40	ale yeast; cold aging; some low esters	DAB Dark, Widmer
20–30	blond alt style; appellation of Cologne (Koln)	Gilden, Muhlen
20–30	smoky flavor from kilned barley	Kaiserdom, Maisel's
8–14	60% wheat; some haze; nose has clove and banana	Hofbrauhaus, Paulaner
8–14	60% wheat; yeast is in bottle to condition	Paulaner Hefe-Weiss
3–8	60% malted wheat; very effervescent, tart; sour	Berliner Kindl Weisse Schultheiss Berliner Weisse
10–15	dark malt	EKU
10–15	40–60% wheat but malty taste	Erdinger, Pinkantus
10–22	lager yeast at ale temperatures ferment with cold-aging	Genesee, Little Kings, Molson Golden
35–45	similar to an IPA, lager yeast at ale temperatures	Anchor, New England Amber

STYLE	ORIGINAL GRAVITY	BODY	COLOR
Ales			
BELGIAN STYLE SPECIALTIES			
Wit	1.044–1.050	M	pale yellow SRM 2–4
Lambic	1.047–1.054	M	yellow to amber SRM 6–15
Belgian Pale	1.048–1.070	L–M	light amber to copper SRM 5–10
Trappist (abbey)	1.060–1.070+	M–F	light (triple) amber (single & double) SRM 10–25
Saison	1.050–1.080	M–F	blonde to to amber SRM 3.5–10
Flanders Brown	1.035–1.053	M	copper to brown SRM 10–30
BELGIAN RED	1.052–1.056	L–M	red SRM 10–18
BELGIAN STRONG	1.060–1.090	L–M	pale to brown SRM 3–35
BIERE DE GARDE	1.060–1.075	M	dark amber SRM 25–40
STRONG SCOTTICH ALES			
Scottish Ale (Strong)	1.072–1.085	F	deep copper to brown SRM 10–45
Old Ale	1.060–1.075	VF	pale to amber SRM 10–16

IBU	CHARACTERISTICS	EXAMPLES
20–30	50% unmalted wheat; tangy; cloudy; some orange and honey (Belgian)	Hoegaarden, Celis
11–22	sour; acidic; uses aged hops; spontaneous ferment in Senne valley of Belgium	Belle-Vue
25–35	low carbonation; fruity; may be dry hopped	Dekonnick
20–40	bottle-conditioned; may use candy sugar; estery	Orval, Chimay
20–30	only 50% attenuated; tart; carbonated laying-down beer	Saison, Dupont
25–40	low hop aroma; sour; spicy; fruity	Liefman's
	low sour; red; fruity	Rodenbach
30	strong alcohol; deceiving body	Lucifer, Duvel
25	malty/fruity aroma; laying-down beer of France; top-fermented	Jenlain
25–35	maltier than Old Ale	McEwans
30–60	low hop aroma; malty	Theakston's

STYLE	ORIGINAL GRAVITY	BODY	COLOR
BITTERS			
Ordinary	1.035–1.038	L–M	gold to amber
Special	1.038–1.042	M	amber to copper
Extra Special	1.042–1.050	F	copper SRM 8–14
PALE ALES			
English Pale	1.044–1.056	M	light copper SRM 6–12
American Pale	1.045–1.056	L–M	pale to copper SRM 4–11
India Pale Ale	1.050–1.064	M	amber to copper SRM 8–18
BROWN ALES			
Mild	1.032–1.036	L	copper to brown SRM 17–34
English Brown Ale	1.040–1.050	M	pale copper to brown SRM 15–22
American Brown Ale	1.040–1.055	M	pale copper to brown SRM 15–22
PORTERS			
Porter Robust	1.045–1.058	M–F	deep with red hues SRM 30+
Brown Porter	1.040–1.050	L–M	deep with red hues SRM 20–35
STOUTS			
Stout Dry	1.038–1.042	L–M	opaque SRM 40+
Foreign	1.050–1.070	L–M	opaque SRM 40+

IBU	CHARACTERISTICS	EXAMPLES
20–25 25–30 30–35	English hops; dry-hopped; usually on draft; northern varieties are more malty; southern are more hoppy	Fullers, Red Hook, Pyramid
20–40	esters noticeable; hoppy nose	Bass, Royal Oak
20–40	less malty than English; higher hops; fruity; uses some crystal	Sierra Nevada, Red Hook
40–60	fruity; maybe some low diacetyl	Anchor Liberty
12–25	malty as possible in a low gravity; very little hop aroma	Grant's Celtic Ale
15–25	northern less sweet than southern; some esters	Watney's Mann's Brown, Newcastle
25–60	drier than English brown; higher hops	Pacific Crest
25–40	low hop aroma; sharp bitterness *without* roast	Anchor, Black Hook
20–30	medium aroma hops	Young's London
30–40	*no* hop flavor or nose, coffee-like	Guinness
30–60	stronger version of dry; similar traits	Guiness Extra

STYLE	ORIGINAL GRAVITY	BODY	COLOR
Sweet	1.038–1.045	M–F	opaque SRM 40+
Oatmeal	1.045–1.056	M–F	opaque SRM 40+
Imperial	1.075–1.095+	F	dark copper+ SRM 20+
BARLEY WINE	1.090–1.120	VF	deep gold-brown SRM 14–40

IBU	CHARACTERISTICS	EXAMPLES
15–25	chocolate-caramel flavor; *no* hop flavor or nose	Mackenson
30–40	variation of sweet using oats; silkiness	Samuel Smith's, New England
50–80+	esters along with high hop flavor and nose	Samuel Smith's
50–100	similar to Old Ale	Thomas Hardy

CHAPTER 4

BEER CHARACTERISTICS

To properly judge a beer and convey the results to other tasters, it is important to have knowledge and mastery of a universal "beer language." Using common terms to communicate helps ensure that judges understand each other when describing the attributes of a beer. The characteristics of appearance, aroma, flavor, and drinkability that follow in this section include basic descriptions of what to observe when tasting or judging a beer. It summarizes what causes each characteristic and examines ways to control each by varying brewing ingredients or procedures.

APPEARANCE

Inspect the bottle before it is opened but don't jump to conclusions. Much can be observed before the beer is opened. Approximately ½ to 1½ inches is usually considered appropriate head space. More than 1½ inches may lead to oxidation, while less than ½ inch can result in gushing. Keep in mind, though, that counter-pressure filled bottles often have less head space than bottle-conditioned beers. Also, when judging appearance, you should consider residue and sediment. The questions to consider when analyzing residue and sediment are: Is there a slight amount of sediment at the bottom of the bottle or a thick layer? Does the sediment cling to the bottom of the bottle? What does this tell the drinker about the care in racking and/or the quality of the yeast? Above and beyond these questions are several important facts. The sediment should be in a thin packed layer. It should be noted that a large amount of sediment can result from careless racking, and a loose bottom layer can occur through mishandling or a poorly flocculating yeast. In commercial examples of lagers and export, there should be no sediment. Filtered or counter-pressure-filled homebrew should have little or no sediment.

Check for a tell-tale bacterial ring around the neck of the bottle at the fill level. Although a small ring may result from the method of priming (see the priming section of this guide), a likely source is a bacterial infection. Gushing is another sign of infection so pay attention to the amount of CO_2 and gushing on opening.

When examining head, the style will dictate whether or not a large, long-lasting head is appropriate. When pouring the beer, try to produce a head approximately 1 inch thick. Some beers, such as stouts and porters, will have less foam or head, whereas wheat beers and Belgian ales will have more foam. In the process, the glass should be poured up to a maximum level of three-quarters full.

In general, all malt beers will produce smaller bubbles and a creamier head. If the bubbles are too big, it could be an indication of either the adjuncts used or an infection. As

A good and practical beer judge will carefully evaluate beer characteristics across a wide spectrum, including: beer appearance, aroma, and flavor. The judge will also make suggestions to the brewer on ways to better the style sample.

a general rule, a bubble which is larger than ¹⁄₁₆" in diameter is too big for malt beers. A rule of thumb is that after one minute at least 50 percent of the head should remain. The appropriate amount of retention is dependent upon the style. (**Note:** Oil, waxes, or dirty glassware can greatly diminish head retention.) "Brussels Lace" is a term used to describe the head that clings to the side of the glass, and is a sign of a fresh, natural beer.

To examine color, hold the sample up to a light. Many judges actually carry a small flashlight with them to assist in their judging of color characteristics. Color should be appropriate for the style being judged. See the style section and the color chart listed later in this book. Look for haze and suspended solids during this phase of your judging. In some styles, such as wit, haze is actually desired. Ales, of course, will generally have more haze than lagers. Chill haze, which appears in a clear beer after it is chilled, may be present because of a shortened protein rest or because of a grain temperature which is too high. Starch haze can be the result of the incomplete conversion of starches to fermentables during the mash. Protein that has not been broken down by the proteolytic enzymes or removed as hot break can be seen as a haze or a rope-like condition in the bottle. Observe the bottle before opening and then the beer in the glass immediately after pouring. Be sure not to introduce any turbidity (the cloudy particles from the yeast layer) as a result of the pour. In addition, be aware that a haze may also be the sign of a bacterial infection.

AROMA/BOUQUET

As in other characteristics, the aroma of a beer depends upon the style of that beer. Lager beers have a flowery and herbal aroma or nose, while ales and wheat beers should leave the impression of fruitiness, and Bavarian beers are noted for their malty bouquet. Immediately after pouring, take several quick sniffs of the beer, swirling the glass between sniffs. Volatile aromas will diminish soon after the pour and thus should be evaluated promptly. The remaining aromas will linger, so after clearing your olfactory senses, take a strong sniff to evaluate the hop nose, the aroma, and the bouquet.

Aroma—This is the sense of the beer's base materials, the raw ingredients of the beer.

Bouquet — The fermentation character of the beer. For example, the fruity or bubblegum notes of esters in heavy ales, or the banana-and-clove-like quality of Bavarian Wheat beers would be described as their respective bouquets.

Hop Nose — The hop characteristic of the beer noted by smell.

Alcohol — Pleasantly fragrant to the nose and perfume-like, this results from a natural chemical group of higher level alcohols called fusel oils. Increased levels of fusel oils are caused by excessive yeast action, high fermentation temperatures, high levels of aminos in the wort, or high ethanol levels. It may also be caused by failure to separate the trub (the hot break and used hops, grain, etc. that lie in the bottom of the brew kettle) from the wort before fermentation.

Light-Struck (skunked)—This unfortunate characteristic occurs when the beer bottles are exposed to ultraviolet light, such as in sunlight or fluorescent lights. Brown bottles give the most protection, but even these only protect a beer in direct sun for several hours.

DMS (cooked corn) — This is the smell of cooked vegetables emanating from the beer. The odor is a product of sulfur compounds, with slow cooling of the wort being the most common cause. Bacteria, *Obesumbacterium proteus,* now called *Hafnia protea,* can also lead to this undesirable characteristic. Strict adherence to sanitation procedures, and quick cooling of the wort is the best line of defense against DMS.

Phenolic—Also referred to as plastic or chlorine, it emits a medicinal smell. Causes of phenolic odors include chlorinated water and insufficient rinsing of equipment sanitized with chlorine. Phenols can also be caused by mutant or wild yeast. Errors of high temperature in the mash or sparging water can extract phenols from the husks of the grain.

Esters — Fruity aromas, such as that of bananas, apples, pears, and pineapples, are the product of aromatic compounds from warm ferments. The fermentation process and type of yeast dictates the production of esters. Ale yeasts are noted for this fruity characteristic. Esters are also produced in high gravity beers. Generally, ales fermented in the 60°F. range will produce less than those in the 70°F. range or higher.

FLAVOR

To evaluate flavor, about a tablespoon of the sample should be sipped and then swirled around in the mouth. Note the flavors on the different parts of your tongue; sweet on the tip, salty to either side in the front, sour to either side toward the back, and bitter on the back middle. Take another sip and observe the mouth feel, then another. With all these, note the effect of aftertaste.

Hoppiness — The bitterness and flavor should match beer profile.

Maltiness — Should be balanced with the hops according to style.

Body — This is also referred to as mouth feel and is rated from light to heavy, once again depending on style.

Carbonation — A mouth feel sensation or texture on the tongue. Low carbonation may be caused by a low priming rate, excessive use of polyclar, cleaning agents, oil, and grease. High carbonation can be caused by overpriming, and through bacterial contamination such as *lactobaccilus*.

Astringent — Also a mouth feel characteristic, but different from bitter; this is dry and puckering. This characteristic is also described as tannic, vinegar, or tart. Astringency is the product of overly-crushed grains (*phenols*), sparging with water which is too hot, hops boiled in the wort too long, and/or poor separation of trub. In the case of hops, the astringent taste would be derived from the pulpy part of the hop, such as bits of stem.

Alcohol — Hot, slightly spicy flavor comes from fusel oils and higher alcohols. Increased levels can result from too high a fermentation temperature and excessive yeast growth.

Phenolic — As with the judging of aroma, this is described as a medicine chest flavor. The causes of this trait are the same as for the phenol aroma and include chlorinated water, chlorine on equipment, tannins extracted from grains by too high a mash temperature, and mutant or wild strains of yeast.

Diacetyl — Diacetyl can be the result of bacterial infections such as *pediococcus*. A butterscotch flavor, this trait is inappropriate in lagers. Yeast both produces and diminishes this trait, which may be caused by racking off the yeast too soon. Warmer fermentations tend to lower this characteristic, thus it is less prevalent in ales. It is also caused by using an increased ratio of adjuncts. Finally, cleanliness, the watchword of brewers, comes to mind as another caveat for diacetyls.

DMS — Commonly referred to as a cooked corn or cooked vegetables quality, its main source is the production of precursors during slow cooling of the wort. Other sources of DMS production include the possibility of a bacterial infection, *Hafnia protea*. Rapid cooling and proper and thorough sanitation procedures are a must in order to avoid DMS. It can also result from precursors known as SMM and DMSO which are complex chemical components formed by problems in the germination and kilning stages of the brewing process.

Estery — This fruity or bubble gum flavor is a character mark of ale yeast. Other sources of an ester flavor include high yeast pitching rates, high fermentation temperatures, and high gravity beers.

Grainy — In commercial beers, this husky characteristic is caused by a high ratio of corn and adjuncts. Homebrewers often encounter this problem from excessive crushing of grain. This flavor can also come from burned grist during decoction mashes.

Metallic — This off-flavor can be the result of iron and other metallic ions in the water supply, or from using mild steel kettles rather than stainless steel.

Nutty — A primary cause of this sherry-like flavor is oxidation or prolonged heating during the aging process. This flavor can be minimized if the brewer avoids aerating the beer during racking and bottling. It can also be prevented by proper air space in the bottle.

Oxidized — This stale paper or cardboard sensation comes from oxygen introduced during the brewing and racking process. It is also caused by storing beer at warm temperatures, which accelerates oxidation.

Solvent — Fermentation at high temperatures causes this acrid, pungent, burning on the tongue. It may also be produced by certain strains of wild yeasts and bacteria that produce high amounts of fatty acids. Temperature control and sanitation are the keys to eliminating solvent-like flavors.

Sour — The most likely cause of this acid flavor is a *lactobacillus* infection. The most common cure is increased attention to the entire sanitation process. This is generally a problem for homebrewers using improperly cleaned equipment and work areas. For example, bottles should be thoroughly sanitized and should be filled only after removing old labels.

Salty — This off-flavor is commonly caused by excessive use of brewing salts or a poor water supply. Brewers with high salts in their water need to find another water supply to use for their brews.

Sweet — The most common cause of this problem is the failure of the yeast to fully ferment the sugars. It is often termed "not fully attenuated." The description "cloyingly sweet" is used when this characteristic is heightened to a level of distraction or discomfort. The brewer can control the sweetness by close monitoring of the mashing procedure. A mash that is not fully complete will yield many non-fermentable dextrins.

Sulphury—This yeasty, rotten egg smell can come from hydrogen sulfide, H_2S, formed by yeast during fermentation. It is generally flushed out by the production of CO_2, with even more driven off by the warm temperatures at which ales ferment. Another source of this problem is mutant yeast strains and several varieties of bacteria, so sanitation procedures are important in order to avoid a sulphur smell. DMS, discussed earlier, is yet another source of sulphur and cooked vegetable smells. Finally, there is the problem of yeast autolysis caused by the yeast digesting itself and releasing hop resins attached to the cell while excreting nitrogen compounds. Yeast autolysis is also described as "rubber-sulfur" by some judges.

Acetaldehyde — Also known as a "cidery" or "green apple" characteristic, this trait occurs naturally in beer from the fermentation process, but usually decreases during aging as the sugar is converted to ethanols. Another cause is the conversion of ethanols to acetaldehyde, caused by bacteria, so sanitation is always a likely culprit. An additional source may be the use of cane or corn sugar in the recipe. A long cold storage is the best method to reduce the acetaldehyde to ethanol.

Grassy—This is a distinct flavor similar to fresh cut grass. This trait is not a common defect, however, and usually comes from the improper storage of grain, generally under warm and humid conditions.

Moldy—This earthy flavor is not a common defect either, however, moldy flavors can be derived from the introduction of fungi, especially if fermenters are located in damp and moldy basements. Most likely, when it does occur, moldy flavor is the result of a sanitation problem.

CHAPTER 5

BREWING INGREDIENTS

Water is the single most important ingredient in beer. Water is also what gives the famous brewing cities some of their unique products. Minerals found naturally in these locations are added as treatments by other brewers hoping to imitate the popular styles. The importance of water cannot be underestimated, therefore brewers give great attention to the ways common minerals and ions affect the brewing process. There are many common minerals and ions used by brewers, too many to be listed. However, the most important of those commonly utilized are:

Gypsum, or Calcium Sulfate, or $CaSO_4$ — Hardens water and is commonly found in the water used in the famous English breweries.

Epsom Salt, or Magnesium Sulfate, or $MgSO_4$ — Another compound used to harden water when duplicating English style ales.

Chalk, or Calcium Carbonate, or CaCO$_3$ — Makes the water hard and alkaline.

WATER

The degree of hardness in water is defined by chemists using two terms: temporary and permanent. Temporary hardness is a term that is used to describe water which contains soluble bicarbonates of calcium and magnesium. These compounds can be removed through boiling which precipitates the carbonates out of solution. Permanent hardness is a term that is used to describe the amount of calcium and magnesium salts in the water. In this form, the magnesium and calcium compounds cannot be removed from the solution.

Hard water is inappropriate for certain styles of beer, such as pilsners. Brewers with only hard water available to them in their area must either find an alternative water supply, change their style of beer, or install water-softening equipment. Clearly, it is very important for the brewer to know the characteristics of his or her water supply before selecting the style of beer he or she wants to brew.

Water has had a significant impact on the styles of beer brewed in different parts of the world. For instance, Munich has carbonate water and therefore naturally tends toward deeper colored beers. Burton, England emerged as the center for pale ales because of the hard water derived from the natural gypsum deposits. The hardness of the water aids in hop utilization. London, alternatively, is the home to English brown ales because the chalkiness of the water lends itself to darker brews in the same manner as it does in Munich. Other regions of Bavaria, on the other hand, have very soft water that is ideal for the softer notes of the finished beer. Dortmund water, finally, is very hard and the resulting beer is a bit darker than a pilsner with a sharper taste than a

Munich. These are but a few examples of how critical it is for the brewer to know the water makeup of his or her area.

Specifically, the measurement of the hardness of water is expressed in parts per million, or PPM. Aside from the hardness of water, there are other characteristics that impact the outcome of the brewers' beer. The most important of these are highlighted for you in detail.

pH is a term that is used to describe the amount of acidity in the water. It is expressed on a scale of 1 to 14, with 7 being neutral, as described in Chapter Two in detail. The low end numbers represent a measure of significant amounts of acid present in the water, while higher numbers represent a certain degree of alkaline in the water. pH is important when mashing grain because, for example, a pH of 5.3 (slightly acidic) is ideal for proteolytic, alpha, and beta amylase enzyme effectiveness. The pH of the water available to a potential brewer also affects the choice of beer to be made, since water with low pH is ideal for lighter colored styles and water with high pH helps to set off the acid in the roasted grains. The pH in any water may be adjusted through the use of ion additions.

Other ions found in water supplies can also have a significant impact on the taste of the finished beer. Calcium releases hydrogen and it is used to lower the pH of a mash to the range of 5.3–5.5 without having to use the natural, and longer, method of an acid rest. This saves time and minimizes the possibility of off-flavors emanating from the husks of the barley. (For more detail, see the Mashing section in Chapter 2 of this book.) Magnesium, although not as effective as calcium, is also used to lower pH. It can, however, impart a sour taste to beer if it reaches concentrations of more than 30 PPM. Sodium additions can provide a round smoothness to the taste, but only in conjunction with the use of chloride. Sodium chloride is commonly known as table salt. When combined with sulfate, it imparts an undesirable harshness.

Bicarbonate has properties which are alkaline and which halt enzyme activity. Unfortunately, bicarbonate can cause problems, extracting harsh flavors from the hops. Alkalinity, however, is not a problem with dark beers, which require an alkaline environment for their success. Sulfate is used in highly hopped beers to attain a sharp, dry edge. However, if sodium is present, the result is a harsh beer. Chloride may hamper the yeast flocculation in the brewing process. While sodium provides roundness, chloride will alternatively wreak havoc with the yeast. Nitrate is not a problem in itself, however the brewer and judge should be aware that bacteria such as *Hafnia protea* can convert nitrate into nitrite, which is harmful since it inhibits yeast metabolism and results in a high level of DMS. (For an explanation of DMS see Beer Characteristics/Aroma in Chapter 4.)

HOPS

Hops are one of the most important flavor characteristics of beer. The botanists' name for hops is *Humulus lupulus.* Hops are a natural member of the family *Cannabinaceae,* a distant cousin of the marijuana plant. Hops are a climbing vine. The hop flower contributes bitterness, aroma, and flavor to beer. Hops also act as a natural preservative for beer. The anatomy of the hop plant is of key importance to the brewer, the judge, and the beer enthusiast. The *storbile* is the term which refers to the whole flower. Resins and essential oils which are responsible for bitterness and aroma are obtained from the *lupulin glands* of the hop flowers. The petals are called *bracteole* with the seeds and lupulin gland located up underneath the bracteole. Hops are plants with gender, thus growers often eliminate the male plants from the hop-yards to minimize the number of seeds.

Rhizomes are shoots which run a few inches underground

and emerge as new plants after root cutting, the traditional method of propagation, is completed. The cutting is usually done in winter, when the plant is dormant, but before the ground is frozen. When uncovering the root, growers look for a large shoot, about ½ inch in diameter. Every few inches along the shoot there should be an area with a bud-like swelling. After finding a rhizome that matches this description, the grower cuts it off near the central root and removes it from the ground. The swelling area or bud is where a new root will appear. The root is cut about 2 inches on either side of this bud and the remaining 4 inch section of rhizome is placed in a plastic bag under refrigeration, until it is planted in the spring.

Rooting is an alternative method of propagation which involves taking a cutting from the new plant as it begins to grow in the spring. As a lateral shoot emerges from the main vine, a cut is made at the base where the shoot has formed three pairs of leaves. The grower removes the bottom pair of leaves from the sprig and roots a new plant in potting soil.

The alpha acid which is a product of the hop flower contributes to the bitterness of the beer. The amount of bitterness is expressed as the percent of

Strobile

Seed

Resin gland

Bracteoles

The Hop Plant

alpha acid in relation to the weight of the flower cone. During boiling, the resin containing the alpha acid *isomerizes* so that the acids become soluble in water. (See isomerization in the Brewing section of Chapter 2.) If not boiled, the acids would merely precipitate out of solution. Beta acids are hop acids which are much more bitter than alpha acids but are nearly insoluble at normal wort pH. The beta acids add very little bitterness to the beer, and what little bitterness they do contribute usually is traced back to oxidation which occurred before the use of hops in the wort.

Essential oils, which are also called hop oils, are responsible for the hop aroma or the character of beer. These are very volatile ingredients and will boil away quickly. Therefore, brewers desiring hop aroma add more hops just before the end of the boil so the aroma is not driven off. Traditional hops of Germany noted for their distinctive aroma are often referred to as noble hops and are popular in many specialty beers.

YEAST

Historically, yeast and bacteria were the least understood aspects of brewing beer. All brewers should now know the major types of yeast and their technical names, along with the differences in the process and the effect each has on the flavor of the beer. The two major types of yeast are *Saccharomyces cerevisia* and *Saccharomyces uvarum*. Each is applied to produce one of the two major groups of beer style, ale, or lagers.

Saccharomyces cerevisia is used in ales and this top-fermenting yeast has a quick ferment and works best at a temperature range of from 50°–75°F. Esters responsible for the fruity aroma characteristics of ales are a major by-product of this yeast. Quite often their aromas are described as smelling like bananas, apples, pears, pineapples, and other

HOP PROFILES				
Types	Alpha percentage {*}	Aroma	Stability	Use
English				
Brewers Gold	8–9	poor	poor	bittering
Bullion	8–9	poor	poor	bittering
Fuggle	4–5	good	fair	flavor/aroma
Kent Goldings	4–5	good	fair	flavor/aroma
Northern Brewer	7–9	fair	fair	bittering
American				
Cascade	4–6	good	poor	flavor/aroma
Chinook	11–14	fair	very good	bitter/aroma
Cluster	6–8	fair	excellent	bittering
Eroica	10–14	fair	fair	bittering
Galena	12–14	poor	very good	bitter/aroma
Mt. Hood	5–7	good	fair	flavor/aroma
Willamette	5–7	good	fair	flavor/aroma
German/Czechoslovakian				
Hallertauer	4–6	good	poor	aroma noble
Hersbrucker	4–6	good	poor	aroma noble
Perle	7–9	good	good	bitter/aroma
Saaz	4–6	good	fair	aroma noble
Tettnang	4–6	good	poor	aroma noble
{*}will vary from one batch of hops to another				

fruits. Another desirable characteristic of ale yeast is its ability to reduce diacetyl, a butter or butterscotch characteristic. This reduction takes place later in the ferment and is one of the marks of a high-quality yeast. Yet another highly valued trait is flocculation, in which the yeast drops to the bottom of the tank after fermentation is complete.

Saccharomyces uvarum (formerly *carlsbergensis)* is used in lagers and this bottom-fermenting lager yeast works best at temperatures of 32°–55°F. Lager yeast is expected to produce very few by-products, therefore, very low levels of esters and diacetyl should be present. Another characteristic of this strain of yeast is a slower ferment at low temperatures, where bacteria cannot function. For this reason, the yeast does not compete with these other organisms. The result is a cleaner beer with very little off flavor. The isolation of lager yeast can be credited to Danish brewer Jacob Christian Jacobsen. Jacobsen wanted to improve the quality of his beers and believed yeast was the answer. Fortunately, his friend was the great Munich brewer Gabriel Sedelmayer from whom Jacobsen secured two casks of yeast and managed to keep the yeast alive on the long journey home. Back in Denmark, at the Carlsberg brewery, laboratory head Emil Hansen was able to isolate a single cell of this strain and determine the characteristics which brewers take for granted today. One method of identifying a lager yeast is its ability to ferment the sugar raffinose, which ale yeast cannot.

Lactobacillus delbrueckii is the strain of yeast that produces the classic Berliner Weisse. It is a combination of top-fermenting yeast and a *lactobacillus* bacteria. A common bacillus would usually result in the runaway breakdown of non-fermentables, but this strain contributes lactic acid without the undesirable side effects. The strain was isolated at the turn of the twentieth century by Professor Max Delbruck, one of the founders of the Institute for Brewing and Fermentation Studies in Berlin which is named in his honor.

Saccharomyces delbrueckii is yet another wheat yeast, this particular strain being used in the Bavarian Weizen style. There is no intentional lactic fermentation in Weizen beer. *Kloeckera apiculata* is a lambic yeast and is one of the many complex components which contributes to the lambic beers. There are other bacteria which can be at work in any given beer. Any of these can and have been used by brewers, but generally add undesirable characteristics to the finished product. For example, *Enterobacteriaceae* or enteric bacteria are lambic strains which occur naturally in the area southwest of Brussels and produce what are normally regarded as off-flavors in most beers. *Brettanomyces bruxellensis* and *lambicus* are another component of lambic and are the wild yeasts from the Senne valley to the southwest of Brussels. The wild yeasts are essential to the spontaneous fermentation of the lambic style and makes this beer nearly impossible to duplicate.

Pediococcus damnosus is another piece of the lambic puzzle which produces lactic acid and some diacetyl.

CLARIFYING AGENTS

Clarifying agents are used by brewers to help clear the beer. They do not add flavor, but rather their main effect is to chemically bond with the compounds that haze beer and then to drop them out of suspension. The following list comprises the most commonly used clarifying agents.

Gelatin — Made from hooves, it clings to yeast, protein, and other large molecules. It is mixed with cold water and allowed to swell. Then, the mixture is warmed enough to dissolve it before adding it to the beer. Proportions are approximately 1 tablespoon per 5 gallons.

Isinglass — This is actually a more pleasant name than its origin which translates "shredded fish bladder membranes." It is used as a clarifier of ale yeast. It is harder to dissolve than gelatin, but is mandatory for beer conditioned in wooden casks.

Irish Moss — Sometimes called "copper fining," Irish moss is a derivative of seaweed. Brewers add it during the boil to aid in the coagulation of proteins. Approximately 1 teaspoon is added in the last 15 minutes of the boil to achieve the optimum effect.

Polyclar — Actually a type of plastic, it is far more effective than other treatments in the reduction of chill haze. Polyclar works through association with its molecular charge. It also seems to help yeast precipitate. A disadvantage is its tendency to reduce head retention. In general, one table-spoon is recommended for every 5 gallons; however, some brewers suggest using up to two tablespoons, particularly in grain brewing.

Bentonite — This is a natural aluminum silicate clay mined in Fort Benton, Montana. It cannot be used in pow-dered form, but must be mixed into a viscous powder/water form called a *slurry*. Sources recommend using a dose of 0.1 to 0.5 parts per thousand.

GRAINS

Barley malt is the most common grain used in brewing. It provides the distinctive flavor identified with beer as well as contributing to its body and alcohol level. Other grains used in the production of beer are called adjuncts. Although rich in starches and sugars, adjuncts will alter the taste of an other-wise fine beer. What follows is an explanation of the malting process, the different types of grains and their properties, and their impact on brewing procedure and styles.

There are two basic types of barley used for brewing, specified by the number of rows of individual grains that emerge from either side of the stem. Each type varies accord-ing to the characteristics found in the anatomy of the grain, so, first, it is important to become familiar with the barley grain itself.

Husk — The husk is the protective covering for each individual barley grain. The thickness and amount of husk varies with the type of barley. A benefit of the husk is the filter bed it forms when lautering during the mashing process. Its negative aspects include harsh flavors and haze caused from tannins.

Acrospire — The formal name for the embryonic plant which grows inside the husk during germination is the acrospire (See Malting in Chapter 2.)

Embryo — This is the growing part of the grain which, if growth is not halted during germination, will develop into a new plant.

Endosperm — The non-living part of the grain which contains the starches (sugars) and proteins (nutrients) used by the yeast for fermentation into beer. With the anatomy of the barley grain in mind, let's now examine the types of barley grain and wheat grain.

Two-Row Barley (*Hordeum distichon*) — This type of grain is more plump than six-row barley. Because each grain is fuller, there is more starch to convert and greater extract yield per weight. The downside inherent in two-row barley is that there is less enzyme potential, although American two-row has more enzymes available than the English varieties. Another disadvantage of two-row barley is its thin husk, which can cause problems when trying to create a proper filter bed during lautering and sparging.

Six-Row Barley (*Hordeum vulgare*) — This grain is easier to grow than two-row barley. Since a higher percentage of this barley is husk and embryo, there is less starch and sugar for fermentation. The husk does provide a good filter bed during lautering and sparging. An undesirable aspect of the larger husk is an increase in tannins (polyphenols) and haze problems. An advantage is the increased number of enzymes for starch conversion.

Wheat (*Triticum Aestivum*) — This is another common grain used to produce distinguished beers, especially in Germany and Belgium. Wheat will impart good heading properties in beer. Unfortunately, the amount of enzymes naturally available in the grain is low. In addition, there are higher levels of protein and a corresponding increase in the likelihood of haze in the finished beer. Wheat is difficult to malt because the acrospire is exposed and can be easily broken off as the grain is turned during malting.

There are several important characteristics in grain that the brewer and judge must consider. Starches and sugars make up the carbohydrates in beer, and this is what the brewer removes from the grain. Starch is the stored food for the embryonic plant and is located in the endosperm. During malting, starch undergoes gelatinization and modification and is transformed into shorter forms of starch that can be effectively used in brewing.

Alpha and beta amylase are natural elements in barley, and it is fortunate that they are, because they are responsible for the conversion of starches to fermentable sugars. (See Malting and Mashing in Chapter 2.) In the mash, they work best at a pH of about 5.3 (slightly acidic) and a temperature of about 154°F. Alpha amylase works by breaking the long starch molecules in the middle of the starch bonds. At the same time, beta amylase works to break the molecules at the ends. The result is a change from starches to sugars that the brewer will eventually ferment into alcohol. *Diastatic power*, which is a measure of the strength of the amylase enzymes present in the grain, is expressed in degrees Lintner. A high number means that there are more enzymes which help to convert the starch into sugars.

Tannins or polyphenols are derived from the husks of grain, and these are a double-edged sword. The husk protects the acrospire during germination but can contribute to several problems such as astringency (harshness) and haze. The tannins will associate with the charge of the long-chain protein molecules. Long enough to refract light, these compounds can produce haze, which is an undesirable characteristic in any style beer.

Amino acids are the building blocks of proteins. The small pieces bonded end to end are molecules called proteins. Small-length aminos are desirable as nutrients for the yeast. Medium length proteins supply roundness and mouth feel

GRAIN SPECIFICATIONS			
Type	° Lovibond	° Lintner	Styles
Low-Kilned Malts (approx. 175°F.)			
6-row Barley	1–2	100–200	American lager, pilsners
2-row Barley	1–2	63–70	lagers
Pale	2–3	36	ales
Malted Wheat	3	49	wheat beer
High-Kilned Malts (approx. 220°F.)			
Mild	3–5	33	mild, brown ale
Vienna	4	30	Dortmunder helles, Bock, Vienna
Munich	6–20	30	Munich
Specialty Malts			
Carapils	1–2	0	light ales
Crystal/Caramel	10–120	0	ales, lagers
Chocolate	300–450	0	dark lagers, dark ales
Black (Patent)	500–1100	0	dark lagers
Adjuncts			
Roasted Barley	500–1100	0	stout, dunkel
Flaked Barley			ales, lagers
Wheat			ales, lagers
Corn			light ale, light lager
Rice			light lagers
Oats			stout, Belgian beer

to the finished beer. However, long proteins contribute to haze and are therefore undesirable. A way to minimize protein haze is to ensure a good rolling boil during brewing. This causes the proteins to vigorously bump into each other and coagulate and then flocculate, resulting in less haze. Proteolytic enzymes occur naturally in grain and also assist in reducing haze by breaking down proteins into smaller amino acids. (See protein rest under Mashing in Chapter 2.) This class of enzymes works best at a pH of about 5.3 and a temperature of approx 122°F.

Degrees Lovibond and SRM (Standard Research Method) are the two systems most commonly used to identify the depth and intensity of malt color.

THE USE OF ADJUNCTS

Adjunct is a term used to define all the grains other than barley that are used to brew beer. Large American brewers use six-row barley because of its increased enzyme content. To combat the haze caused by the additional tannins of six-row, brewers use corn, rice, and oats, which have no polyphenols and almost no proteins. Another advantage to the use of adjuncts is the high amount of starch content present and the lower cost of using these grains, when compared to barley malt. Thus, American brewers who use adjuncts produce a very pale beer, which, until recently, has been the favorite of the American beer drinker. The biggest disadvantages to beers produced with adjuncts are the off-flavors and the rough taste, which is sometimes described as grainy.

Today, however, much to the chagrin of the large brewers who use adjuncts to mass produce the pale beers, Americans' tastes seem to be changing, moving in the direction of higher-quality boutique beers. This movement is most evident in the enormous sales increases presently being enjoyed by microbrewers and brewpubs across the country. These microbrewers and brewpubs are producing beers which utilize only the highest quality malts, hops, and waters and which contain no adjuncts. The American beer enthusiast is certainly beginning to show a renewed respect for the time, care, expense, and knowledge of the smaller brewers who are producing some of the best products America has ever put in a beer glass.

In this book, you will find a comprehensive directory of the microbreweries and brewpubs across the United States. I encourage you to take to the road, experience these great products, and utilize your new-found knowledge of beer styles and beer judging to rank your preferences. There is a whole world of wonderful beer out there, in your state, in your city, in your neighborhood, and on your vacation route, just waiting for you.

BEER STYLES AND HOPS		
Beer Styles	**Bittering/Flavor**	**Aroma/Finish**
American Lagers	Clusters, Cascade, Willamette, Saaz	Cascade, Hallertauer,
European Lagers	Hallertauer, Saaz, Tettnang, Spalt, Bavarian Northern Brewer	Saaz, Hallertauer, Tettnang
Wheat Beers	Clusters, Eroica, Tettnang	Hallertauer
English Ales	Northern Brewer, Goldings, Fuggles, Cascade, Cluster, Chinook	Kent Goldings, Cascade, Hallertauer, Fuggles
Porter	Northern Brewer, Chinook	Cascade
Steam	Northern Brewer, Cascade, Chinook	Northern Brewer, Cascade
Kriek	Cluster	N/A
Stein	Northern Brewer	Hallertauer

CHAPTER 6

PREPARING FOR THE BJCP EXAM

So, you ask, why are guidelines required for tasting? You may think all that's needed is to lift the glass, pour it down, and there— it's tasted. Well, not exactly, although millions of beer drinkers do make decisions in a manner similar to this. This section will explore the method used to make knowledgeable evaluations of various types of beers. The goal is to taste beers and, even if the style is not of a personal preference, to make a rational and communicable judgment on the quality of the beer.

The process starts with the selection of equipment. As with any endeavor, the correct materials can make a world of difference.

GLASSWARE

There are several factors to consider when planning and organizing a tasting. A good starting point is the choice of glasses. Many experts suggest the use of brandy snifters. This stemware will provide access to all the characteristics the taster needs to observe. Other glassware, such as wine glasses, may also be suitable if, like the snifter, they have the following attributes:

1. The glasses are made of clear glass, to provide an easy check of the beer color and clarity.

2. The glasses allow the taster/judge to hold the glass by the stem and maintain the chill, or, to cup the bowl of the glass and warm an over-chilled sample.

3. The glasses provide a well to encase and hold the aroma and bouquet released from the beer.

Care should always be taken to guard the glasses from anything that will potentially taint the beer. Set the glasses aside and designate them "for beer only." Residues from juice and other drinks could be retained on the surface or in small defects and mar the performance of an otherwise respectable beer glass.

Be sure the glasses are thoroughly cleaned by a good detergent that does not have an animal fat base. Oils and fats can leave residues which will ruin head retention. For this reason, you should also avoid soaps, sponges, washrags, and anything else which can contain an oily or greasy substance when cleaning or handling your tasting glasses. A common and useful recommendation is to use a cleaning solution made of hot water and baking soda. Rinse the glasses completely and allow to air dry. In the case of large tastings or judgings, the sheer volume of glasses needed may be prohibitive. In these instances, organizations often use a high-quality, clear hard plastic which is smooth-sided. A six-ounce size is usually sufficient for tasting purposes.

SELECTION OF BEERS

A judge is generally expected to evaluate one style of beer with up to ten different samples of that particular style category. An informal tasting should have no more than ten samples of any particular style, category or combination, since more than ten samples may cause confusion. In a casual rating session, a variety of styles may be present, since this approach usually heightens enjoyment of the event. In these situations, the beers are arranged in a spectrum, with the lighter styles being tasted first and gradually progressing to the more full-bodied samples at the conclusion. Judges in smaller competitions who may be assigned to span two or three categories, or participate in a "best of show," must also consider this sequencing.

The time of day is another important factor when considering a tasting event. Late morning, after the taste and flavors of breakfast have faded and an approaching midday hunger has aroused the appetite, is the most agreed upon time for accurate tasting. This is precisely the time most judging competitions commence. A suitable alternative, for the same reasons, is just before the evening meal. Oily and spicy foods, and actually any food, can affect taste buds and, therefore, eating should be delayed until after the tasting event. For an informal tasting, the camaraderie and social atmosphere of the process is an excellent lead-in to dinner.

A room that is well-lit, ventilated, and cool is ideal for beer tasting. The air should be clean. Cigarette and other smoke should be discouraged, since these can inhibit the judges' ability to detect the nuances of beer aroma and bouquet. Good lighting and, if possible, white table cloths will help with the evaluation of color and clarity. Some tasters/judges bring a small flashlight to assist them in the criticism of color and clarity.

There are some auxiliary items that make a tasting go smoothly. These items include bottle openers, napkins, pencils, score-sheets, plain, unflavored crackers, plain bread, and plenty of water, sometimes sparkling water. The water and crackers are useful, because they help cleanse the palate between samples. If crackers are used, select a type that is low in both salt and fat, to lessen the effect on taste. Even with low-salt, low-fat crackers, many tasters and judges observe that all crackers, regardless of how mild, can leave a yeasty, background flavor that interferes with an accurate assessment of the beer. It is a personal preference, but for this reason plenty of water is accepted as the best way to cleanse the palate.

RATING THE BEER

Many different versions of scoring are available and endorsed by beer experts. For competitions, the American Homebrewers Association in Colorado, one of the leading tasting and judging organizations in the country, has endorsed a standardized 50-point system. For novices, this has the potential to be a bit intimidating. Other sources, such as Charlie Papazian, Fred Eckhardt, and Dave Miller, among the leaders in the tasting and judging of U.S. beers, recommend a simple 20-point system distributed among four categories. This system breaks down as follows:

1. Appearance...........0–3 points
   - Clarity
   - Color

2. Aroma...................0–4 points
   - Aroma, from fermentables
   - Bouquet, from hops

3. Taste....................0–10 points

   - Balance, hops and malt

   - Mouth feel, body

   - Aftertaste

4. Overall impression.......1–3 points

The score sheets should contain enough room for the judges to write notes on their observations. The beers are judged, not in comparison to one another, but in comparison to the style profiles. (See Chapter 3 on Styles.) For those studying to take the Beer Judge Certification Exam, it is more appropriate to use the American Homebrewers Association competition score sheet. (This AHA scoring system appears in Appendix 2.)

POURING THE BEER

The appeal of light-tasting beers has resulted in serving most other beer styles too cold, especially in America! Do not fall into this trap when holding a tasting. A beer that is over-chilled will not release and reveal its true character. The subtleties of aroma and taste will be hidden in the too cold beer, just as surely as they would in a frozen French pastry. The actual recommended temperatures at which beers should be consumed are shown in the box at right.

These temperatures may be rather difficult to maintain, since the average refrigeration equipment has temperatures which hover in the 34°–37°F. range. A realistic average temperature to shoot for is about 50°–60°F.; cooler for lighter styles and warmer for darker beers. If you pull the beers out of the

RECOMMENDED TEMPERATURES

Pale lagers	45°–50°F.
Amber/dark lagers	50°–55°F.
Pale ales	50°–55°F.
Dark ales, Stouts	55°–60°F.

refrigerator and let them sit for 10–15 minutes, you will be more likely to attain the correct temperature range. Another option is to pour the refrigerated beer, then microwave it for a few seconds, until the desired temperature is achieved.

Also helpful is an inexpensive refrigerator temperature control device, for use on that second refrigerator some judges are lucky enough to have in the basement!

At private tastings and competitions, judges will often pour the beer into a pitcher with one smooth pour down the side, then pass the pitcher around. This becomes important if there are more than four tasters.

Prior to opening the beer, check the condition of the bottle. Is the air space at the top of the bottle correct? Remember, it should be ½–1½ inches. Are there signs of infection? This would be indicated by a small ring at the fill level. Is there haze? Most beer styles should not have haze if the mashing and brewing were done properly. Is the sediment layer thin and tightly packed? If so, good yeast was used and correct racking and handling procedures were followed. When opening the bottle, does the carbonation sound right? It should wisp open, but not gush.

If the beer is bottle-conditioned, there will be a thin layer of yeast sediment at the bottom. Thus, the beer should be decanted with one continuous pour. The bottle can be held tilted, but should not be returned upright until pouring is complete. Stop the pour before any sediment passes out the neck of the bottle.

To begin pouring, splash some beer down the center of the glass and quickly determine the amount of carbonation. Then, either continue down the middle, to encourage the formation of head, or minimize head by pouring gently down the side. The correct pour leaves a glass that is ⅔ full with a collar of head ½–1½ inches thick. At this point, the evaluation has already started.

AROMA AND BOUQUET

Although much useful information about the beer has already been gathered and there is a temptation to start writing notes, now is not the time for hesitation. Immediately after the pour, quickly raise the glass and smell the sample. Beer contains volatile aromas that must be evaluated without delay. Volatile means that those substances will not remain in solution at drinking temperatures and higher. Even at these low temperatures, they readily evaporate into vapors. So, sniff the beer quickly a couple of times, swirl the glass, then take a couple more quick sniffs.

Now pause, since your nose may have become accustomed to the smell. Contemplate the aroma from the natural ingredients and bouquet of the overall smell from fermentation. Then, record your impressions. During this period, start observing the color and clarity of the brew.

APPEARANCE

Hold the glass up to the light. Does the color fit the style? Should the beer be clear or, as in wheat beer, is a little cloudiness acceptable? A thorough knowledge of beer types, a reference color chart, and a description of individual styles can greatly aid the judging during this portion of tasting. The comments gathered from this inspection should be combined with the observations noted during pouring. The judges' remarks should be written down, along with the award of points for the faithful replication of style.

Take a good look at the head and gas release of the beer. Is the head the correct color? For example, a wheat beer should be very white, while a stout will have a creamy beige or light brown head. Are the bubbles small and densely packed in an even distribution? A thick long-lasting head of small bubbles points to the use of all natural ingredients and natural carbonation, in place of sugar priming or CO_2 injection. A general guideline for head retention is that more than half of the head should be present after one minute. Record all your comments at this time.

Following the evaluation of appearance, the olfactory senses should have cleared. This is a good time to repeat the sniffing and swirling. Are there any off odors? If so, check the characteristics, in Chapter 4 of this book, and make appropriate notes on the score sheet. Be sure to consider how this will impact the aroma score for the sample.

FLAVOR

Finally! Who'd have ever known that so much thought would be required just to properly taste a beer! But the process is not over. At this stage, only three out of five senses have been used. Now it's time to employ the other two.

Pick up the glass and slowly bring it to the lips, allowing the aroma and bouquet to envelope the nose. Sip about 1–1½ tablespoons of the beer. Feel the carbonation and swish the beer around to cover all parts of the mouth. Note which parts of the tongue are stimulated: sweet on the tip, salt to either side in the front, bitter in the back, sour on each side toward the back. Closing the eyes at this point can eliminate distractions and help the judge to concentrate the sensory experience on touch and taste. Try drawing air in through the beer to warm it and release flavors. As you finish swallowing, part the lips with a slight inhalation that will aerate the beer and stimulate the olfactory area.

After waiting a moment, take another sip. This time, pay attention to the mouth feel. Some judges like to "chew" the sample. Is the beer full or thin? Does it come across as bitter or sweet? Are the bubbles numerous and distracting, and are they large or small? Does the beer have that puckering feeling

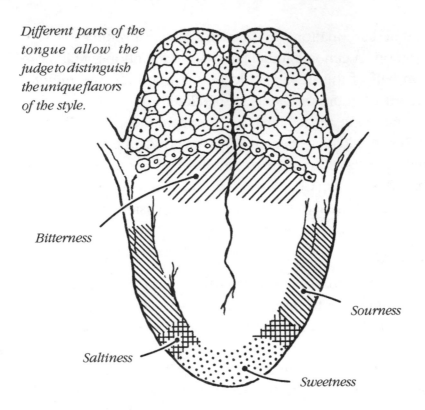

Different parts of the tongue allow the judge to distinguish the unique flavors of the style.

Bitterness

Sourness

Saltiness

Sweetness

along the inside of your lower lip that is associated with astringency? Take note of these and compare them with the ideal style characteristics.

Yet another sip is in order. Try to separate the taste of hops and malt. Is each appropriate for the style? With practice, tasters can distinguish the differences between the hop bitterness and flavor, and whether they are correct for the type of beer. What about the hops-to-malt balance; is it appropriate? By this stage a fairly complete picture has developed and a large base of facts is available for jotting down impressions. Get these down on the score sheet while continuing to compare and contrast the beer with the style profile.

At the end of an informal tasting, gather the results and share impressions. Discussions will naturally flow about observations, personal preference, appealing traits and subtle differences. For the beer judge, this is only part of the process. The added responsibilities of judging are designed for a higher purpose — a better beer.

JUDGING

Judges follow all the actions outlined for tasting, but in evaluating the beers, judges observe a shift in the emphasis. The goal of judging is to provide feedback that will assist the brewer in refining his or her technique and the replication of styles. There are two cardinal rules to follow:

1. The judge focuses on comments that will help the brewer.

2. The judge finds at least one good thing to say about every beer.

The challenge in judging is making knowledgeable comparisons to standardized profiles and ranking the entries in some order. In the process of evaluating, the judge is called upon to:

1. Compare the beer to existing styles.

2. Identify the strong points of the beer.

3. Offer tactful, concise suggestions to the brewer to help overcome flaws.

4. Provide consistent scoring.

5. Communicate all the above effectively to other judges and brewers.

Although it is not possible for each judge to be an expert in every beer type, it should be a judge's objective to continuously expand his or her knowledge base and to feel comfortable and competent judging across a number of styles. However, a judge should be very honest with competition organizers about which areas are his or her weaknesses. Judges must actively continue their own education in identifying beer faults and explaining the variety of actions brewers can take to refine their processes. Continuing to expand one's knowledge means to:

1. Read, refresh, and study beer styles and profiles.

2. Practice tasting and scoring commercial beers representing specific styles.

3. Regularly review beer faults, causes, and corrective actions.

4. Actively participate as a judge.

5. Communicate with other judges and brewers.

Finally, it is also a judge's duty to act as a mentor for the stewards, and for apprentice judges. Stewards are those people who assist in the logistics of a competition. Today's stewards are not just beer gophers and score sheet collectors; they are tomorrow's judges. Spend time discussing the style, what will be looked for, and what role the steward will fill. After each entry is judged, consider allowing the steward to taste the beer and fill out an unofficial score sheet. Discuss the traits, attributes, and other characteristics of the beer, and compare the official score to the steward's. This will further the training of a potential judge and provide invaluable experience for the steward.

There are certain items a judge may want to have available at the competition. Not all contests are equally organized, thus a judge may wish to prepare a portable judging kit. The contents of this pack would include such things as:

1. A small flashlight for use in evaluating color and clarity.

2. A small white napkin or handkerchief to place the entry on when observing color, in case white tablecloths are not used.

3. Extra pencils and erasers. Yes, even judges can make mistakes. Mechanical pencils with extra lead often work best.

4. This reference book, which contains descriptions of styles and faults. Also keep handy the descriptions provided to you at the start of the competition.

5. A copy of the Beer Judge Certification Program guidelines.

6. Extra copies of competition score sheets.

In actual judging, the actions and procedures are similar to what was outlined in the tasting section of this chapter. The notes on attributes and suggestions for improvement of the beer are then placed in the appropriate section of the score sheet.

When using the American Homebrewers Association (AHA) standardized scoring system, rate each characteristic under the headings of Bouquet/Aroma, Appearance, Flavor, Body. Then, go back and add these ratings to get the score for each heading. Decide on a target number and review comments to be sure the score and comments match. The overall impression area is a place where minor adjustments can be made to attain the target number.

DEFINITIONS OF AHA SCORES

Excellent	40-50
Very Good	30-39
Good	25-29
Drinkable	20-24
Problem	19

It is not advisable to give any beer a score lower than a 19. Remember, the purpose of the competition is to *help* the brewer overcome problems, refine procedures, and replicate classic styles. These three objectives should guide the content of the written remarks. A minimum score of 19 is surely a sufficient statement. There is no need to humiliate the brewer. After all, the basis of the American Homebrewers Association is encouragement and assistance of those interested and involved in the brewing industry.

BEER JUDGE CERTIFICATION PROGRAM

The Beer Judge Certification Program was initiated to achieve a higher level of consistency in judging and to raise the overall quality of homebrewing. Founded in 1985, the program to certify beer judges is a joint effort sponsored by the AHA and the HWBTA (Home Wine and Beer Trade Association). Each organization appoints a co-director for the writing, administration, and grading of the exam. The purpose of the exam is to identify and recognize those brewers and beer enthusiasts who have attained the knowledge to identify classic beer styles, and who have the ability to make constructive comments for the improvement of brewing.

The certification and testing process evaluates the person's knowledge of brewing history, beer flavor, and aroma profiles, the characteristics of accepted beer styles, and the brewing process. A major emphasis of the BJCP is continuing education and progression through increasing levels of judging ability. The examination consists of two parts and

---

REQUIRED EXAMINATION SCORE AND EXPERIENCE

Level	Exam Score	Minimum Experience points
Recognized	60	0 (none needed for this entry level)
Certified	70	5 (2.5 must be judging points)
National	80	20 (10 must be judging points)
Master	90	40 (20 must be judging points)

Honorary Master This is a temporary designation awarded by a BJCP committee to a recognized expert. BJCP directors also hold this level designation during their term. Experience points are gained through participation in program events. The amount of points are based on the responsibility in and size of the competition. Several definitions are necessary for explaining the award of experience points including the size of the competition.

---

lasts three hours. The written section is comprised of ten questions and is 70 percent of the grade. The tasting section, worth 30 percent of the final exam grade, consists of up to four beers that are presented throughout the written portion. Grading is based upon ability to identify correct profiles and strong points of the beer while being able to tactfully suggest improvements.

Judges progress through levels by meeting requirements of a minimum exam score (see box above) and a combination of judging and non-judging experience points (see boxes, pages 100-101).

Competitions are categorized by size as follows: National Competition — Annual AHA, HWBTA competitions open to all homebrewers. Large Regional — Open competitions which draw 75 entries or more. Small Regional — Open competitions which draw under 75 entries. Judging will earn experience points by the schedule of:

Small Regional = 0.5 points

Large Regional = 1.0 points

National = A maximum of 5 points for both rounds
of the national competition.

Additional points are earned by judging in a competition's Best of Show. This round of judging is comprised of the first place beers from each category. Experience points for Best of Show judging are higher, based on the difficulty of judging the wide variety of styles present in the Best of Show round. Competitions that attract at least six entries in each of five different categories are eligible to award Best of Show points. There may be one Best of Show judge appointed for every 25 entries, up to a maximum of four Best of Show judges for each competition.

JUDGING BEST OF SHOW EXPERIENCE

The points awarded for this category are:

Small Regional = 1.0 points (less than 75 entries)

Large Regional = 2.0 points (more than 75 entries)

Each judging level has a maximum number of experience points that can be earned in support of the program outside of actual judging. There are several ways to earn these points.

ORGANIZER POINTS

Entries	Non-judging experience points
1–74	2
75–149	3
150–299	5
300–499	7
over 500	10

ORGANIZER POINTS

Non-judging experience points are awarded to organizers of competitions. The number earned is based upon the total entries to be judged. (See box at left.) Those who act as an assistant organizer also receive non-judging points based on entries. (See box at right.)

In addition, non-judging points can be earned through distribution of points from the two organizer categories. A Steward, Judge, or Best of Show Judge may receive up to one organizer or assistant organizer point allocated by the organizer. The organizer may allocate organizing and assistant organizer points between staff members in 0.5 point increments.

Additional non-judging experience points can be earned as a steward. These points are based on the size classification of the competition. (See box at right.)

If circumstances prevent a BJCP co-director from being present at an examination, the co-directors may appoint a qualified person to administer and proctor the exam. Judges appointed to this task can earn additional non-judging points based on the number of examinees. (See box at right.)

The judge who administers the exam and earns these points can allocate them to people that assist in exam administration in increments of no less than 0.5 points.

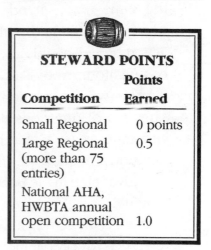

ASSISTANT ORGANIZER POINTS

Entries	Non-judging experience points
150–299	1
300–499	3
500 or more	5

STEWARD POINTS

Competition	Points Earned
Small Regional	0 points
Large Regional (more than 75 entries)	0.5
National AHA, HWBTA annual open competition	1.0

JUDGES POINTS

Examinees	Non-judging experience points
4–6	0.5
7–11	1
more than 11	2

PREPARATIONS FOR THE EXAM

The planning and announcement of the exam is usually done at least two months prior to the test date, so use this time wisely. Begin by sampling commercial styles of the beer categories. Use a listing of style descriptions and take notes on your observations of each sample. This is part of taste training and will help you learn the profiles of each type. At the same time, attend local homebrewers' meetings and become acquainted with the various faults and corrective actions. If possible, serve as a steward at a sanctioned competition. Above all, know the style profiles.

The written portion of the exam usually contains a sampling of questions on styles, brewing procedures, malt and grain, yeast, water, hops, the history of brewing, and a question that addresses the procedure for becoming a judge and advancing in the Beer Judge Certification Program. Keep in mind, however, that the exam format does change from year to year, so be fully prepared. This book is a good reference for preparation. The bibliography contains other books that are also helpful study guides. The study and prep time should be systematically spread out over this entire period. Perhaps the biggest error in getting ready is cramming the night before. Cramming does not follow the program's philosophy of continuous education and improvement. As with any exam, drinking prior to the BJCP exam is not recommended, since residual alcohol could inhibit your performance.

There are several things you can do to prepare for examination day.

1. Ensure proper mouth condition on the morning of the exam, and before all beer tasting. Thoroughly

floss and brush teeth. Brushing should include the tongue and roof of the mouth.

2. Avoid fruits and sweets, fats, oils, and spicy foods, as these adversely affect taste. Do be sure to have a good meal before the exam, since you will be taking a 3 hour test and drinking several beers before you have a chance to eat again.

3. Gather materials that will be helpful during the exam, such as pencils, paper clips, paper, a flashlight, and a handkerchief.

4. Bring some bottled water for clearing your palate in case it's needed.

5. On starting the examination, read through all the questions quickly, before writing anything. Determine if there are any areas of overlap and how to approach these.

6. Ten questions in three hours does not necessarily equate to 18 minutes per question. Some will take longer, some less. Try to plan approximately how long you will spend on each question.

7. Even if a question causes you to draw a blank, demonstrate at least your broad-based knowledge. This will at least afford you the possibility of acquiring additional points.

These preparation tips basically advise you to use the same common sense that you would prior to any important exam. Be sure to allow yourself ample time to answer the written questions in a well-organized manner, to judge the beers carefully, and to pay attention to your spelling and handwriting. If your answers aren't legible, you don't pass.

CONCLUSION

There are over 200 brands and 70 styles of beer commercially available today. As a beer enthusiast myself, I invite you to join me in the ongoing process of learning about the brewing process, the ingredients, and the various beer styles. Ultimately, I invite you to get involved in judging some of these great products from around the world. Beer, whether brewed by the largest brewery in Germany, or by the smallest homebrewer in the United States, is a drink to be respected, shared, and enjoyed among friends and fellow enthusiasts. I hope the information I have presented to you in my book helps you in your continuing education involving beers from around the world. *Prosit!*

APPENDIX ONE

COLOR DEFINITIONS
SRM (STANDARD RESEARCH METHOD)

Color	SRM number
Water	0.0
Light straw	1–2.5
Pale straw	2.5–3.5
Dark straw	3.5–5.5
Light amber	5.5–10
Pale amber	10–18
Dark amber or copper	18–26
Very dark amber	26–40
Black	40+

Note: Some sources use the European system, called EBC (European Brewing Convention scale). To convert from EBC to SRM, multiply the EBC number by 0.375, then add 0.46.

BEER SCORE SHEET (FALL 1993)

DESCRIPTOR DEFINITIONS

✔ **CHECK WHENEVER APPROPRIATE**

☐ **Acetaldehyde**—Green applelike aroma; byproduct of fermentation.

☐ **Alcoholic**—The general effect of ethanol and higher alcohols. Tastes warming.

☐ **Astringent**—Drying, puckering (like chewing on a grape skin) feeling often associated with sourness. Tannin. Most often derived from boiling of grains, long mashes, oversparging or sparging with hard water.

☐ **Bitter**—Basic taste associated with hops; braun-hefe or malt husks. Sensation experienced on back of tongue.

☐ **Chill haze**—Haze caused by precipitation of protein-tannin compound at cold temperatures. Does not affect flavor Reduction of proteins or tannins in brewing or fermenting will reduce haze.

☐ **Chlorophenolic**—Caused by chemical combination of chlorine and organics. Detectable in parts per billion. Aroma is unique but similar to plasticlike phenolic. Avoid using chlorinated water.

☐ **Cooked Vegetable/Cabbagelike**—Aroma and flavor often due to long lag times and wort spoilage bacteria that later are killed by alcohol produced in fermentation

☐ **Diacetyl/Buttery**—Described as buttery, butterscotch Sometimes caused by abbreviated fermentation or bacteria.

☐ **DMS** (dimethyl sulfide)—A sweet, cornlike aroma/flavor Can be attributed to malt, short or non-vigorous boiling of wort, slow wort chilling or, in extreme cases, bacterial infection.

☐ **Fruity/Estery**—Similar to banana, raspberry, pear, apple or strawberry flavor; may include other fruity/estery flavors Often accentuated with higher temperature fermentations and certain yeast strains.

☐ **Grainy**—Raw grain flavor. Cereallike. Some amounts are appropriate in some beer styles.

☐ **Hoppy**—Characteristic odor of the essential oil of hops Does not include hop bitterness.

☐ **Husky**—See Astringent.

☐ **Light-Struck**—Having the characteristic smell of a skunk, caused by exposure to light Some hops can have a very similar character.

☐ **Metallic**—Caused by exposure to metal. Also described as tinny, coins, bloodlike. Check your brewpot and caps.

☐ **Oxidized/Stale**—Develops in the presence of oxygen as beer ages or is exposed to high temperatures, winy, wet cardboard, papery, rotten vegetable/pineapple, sherry, baby diapers. Often coupled with an increase in sour, harsh and bitter. The more aeration in bottling/siphoning or air in headspace, the more quickly a beer will oxidize. Warm temperatures dramatically accelerate oxidation.

☐ **Phenolic**—Can be any one or combination of a medicinal, plastic, electrical fire, Listerinelike, Band-Aidlike, smoky, clovelike aroma or flavor. Most often caused by wild strains of yeast or bacteria. Can be extracted from grains (see astringent). Sanitizing residues left in equipment can contribute.

☐ **Salty**—Flavor associated with table salt. Sensation experienced on sides of tongue. Can be caused by presence of too much sodium chloride, calcium chloride or magnesium sulfate (Epsom salts); brewing salts.

☐ **Solventlike**—Flavor and aromatic character of certain alcohols, often due to high fermentation temperatures Like acetone, lacquer thinner.

☐ **Sour/Acidic**—Pungent aroma, sharpness of taste. Basic taste like vinegar or lemon; tart. Typically associated with lactic or acetic acid. Can be the result of bacterial infection through contamination or the use of citric acid. Sensation experienced on sides of tongue.

☐ **Sweet**—Basic taste associated with sugar. Sensation experienced on front tip of tongue.

☐ **Sulfurlike(H_2S; Hydrogen sulfide)**—Rotten eggs, burning matches. Is a byproduct with certain strains of yeast Fermentation temperature can be a factor of intensity Diminishes with age. Most evident with bottle-conditioned beer.

☐ **Yeasty**—Yeastlike flavor. Often due to strains of yeast in suspension or beer sitting on sediment too long.

Round No. _____ Entry No. _____

Category No. _____

Subcategory (spell out) _____

Judged By (please print) _____

Judge Qualifications (check one): ☐ Recognized ☐ Certified
☐ National ☐ Master ☐ Experienced (but not in BJCP)
☐ Apprentice or Novice ☐ Other: _____

BOTTLE INSPECTION Comments _____

_____

_____

	Max. Score
BOUQUET/AROMA (as appropriate for style)	10 _____

Malt (3), Hops (3), Other Aromatic Characteristics (4)

Comments _____

_____

_____

_____

_____

APPEARANCE (as appropriate for style)	6 _____

Color (2), Clarity (2), Head Retention (2)

Comments _____

_____

_____

_____

FLAVOR (as appropriate for style)	19 _____

Malt (3), Hops (3), Conditioning (2), Aftertaste (3), Balance (4), Other Flavor Characteristics (4)

Comments _____

_____

_____

_____

_____

_____

_____

BODY (full or thin as appropriate for style)	5 _____

Comments _____

_____

_____

_____

_____

DRINKABILITY & OVERALL IMPRESSION	10 _____

Comments _____

_____

_____

_____

_____

TOTAL (50 possible points): _____

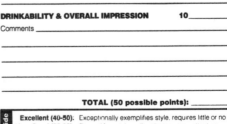

Scoring Guide

Excellent (40-50):	Exceptionally exemplifies style, requires little or no attention
Very Good (30-39):	Exemplifies style well, requires some attention
Good (25-29):	Exemplifies style satisfactorily, but requires attention
Drinkable (20-24):	Does not exemplify style, requires attention
Problem (<20):	Problematic, requires much attention

Use other side for additional comments. © AHA/SCP 4/93

American Homebrewers Association • PO Box 1679 • Boulder • CO 80306-1679 • (303) 447-0816 • FAX (303) 447-2825

APPENDIX THREE

Homebrew Supply Shops

ALASKA

Alaska Mill Feed & Garden
Center
1501 E. 1st Avenue
Anchorage, AK 99501
(907) 276-6016

ARIZONA

Brewmeisters Supply Co.
1924 W. Aster Drive
Phoenix, AZ 85029
(602) 843-4337

CALIFORNIA

Barley and Wine Home
Fermentation Supply
1907 Central Avenue
Ceres, CA 95307
(209) 538-BREW

Bayside Brewing Supply
2977 Bayside Lane
San Diego, CA 92109
(619) 488-8185

Beer Makers of America
San Jose, 1040 N. 4th Street
San Jose, CA 95112
(408) 288-6647

The Beverage People
840 Piner Road, #14
Santa Rosa, CA 95403
(800) 544-1867
(707) 544-2520 (advice line)

The Fermentation Settlement
1211 C Kentwood Avenue
San Jose, CA 95129
(408) 973-8970

Fermentation Frenzy
991 N. San Antonio Road
Los Altos, CA 94022
(415) 941-9289

Great Fermentations of Marin
87 Larkspur
San Rafael, CA 94901
(800) 570-BEER

The Home Brewery
738 S. Waterman Ave., #B-28
San Bernardino, CA 92408
(800) 451-MALT
(909) 888-7746

Napa Fermentation Supplies
724 California Blvd.
Napa, CA 94559
(800) 242-8585
(707) 255-6372

Old River Brew Co.
8524 Old River Road
Bakersfield, CA 93311
(805) 398-0454

Portable Potables
1011 41st Avenue
Santa Cruz, CA 95062
(408) 476-5444

R & R Home Fermentation
Supplies
8385 Jackson Road
Sacramento, CA 95826
(916) 383-7702

SLO Home Brew Supply
383½ Lemon Street
San Luis Obispo, CA 93401
(805) 544-2064

St. Patrick's of California Brewer's
Supply
616 California Street
Santa Cruz, CA 95060
(408) 459-0178

The WineSmith
346 Main Street
Placerville, CA 95667
(916) 622-0516

COLORADO

The BREW-IT Company
120 West Olive Street
Fort Collins, CO 80524
(800) 748-2226
(303) 484-9813

Liquor Mart
1750 15th Street
Boulder, CO 80302
(303) 449-3374

What's Brewin'
1980 8th Street
Boulder, CO 80302
(303) 444-9433

Wine & Hop Shop
705 E. 6th Avenue
Denver, CO 80203
(303) 831-7229

The Wine Works
5175 W. Alameda Avenue
Denver, CO 80219
(303) 936-4422

CONNECTICUT

Brew & Wine Hobby
68 Woodbridge Avenue
East Hartford, CT 06108
(203) 528-0592 (in CT)
(800) 352-4238 (outside CT)

The Mad Capper
P.O. Box 310126
Newington, CT 06131-0126
(203) 667-7662

S.E.C.T. Brewing Supply
C/O SIMTAC
20 Attawan Road
Niantic, CT 06357
(203) 739-3609

Wine and Beer Art of Smith
Tompkins
1501 E. Main Street, Route 202
Torrington, CT 06790
(203) 489-4560

DELAWARE

Wine Hobby USA
2306 W. Newport Pike
Stanton, DE 19804
(800) 847-HOPS
(302) 998-8303

FLORIDA

Home Brewer's Outlet
4345 Okeechobee Blvd.,
Building F-5
West Palm Beach, FL 33409
(800) 644-5555

The Home Brewery
416 S. Broad Street
P.O. Box 575
Brooksville, FL 34605
(800) 245-BREW
(904) 799-3004

GEORGIA

Wine Craft of Atlanta
3400 Wooddale Drive N.E.
Atlanta, GA 30326
(404) 266-0793

ILLINOIS

Alternative Garden Supply, Inc.
297 N. Barrington Road
Streamwood, IL 60107
(800) 444-2837
(708) 885-8282

Fleming's Winery
RR2, Box 1
Oakwood, IL 61858
(800) 832-4292
(217) 354-4555

Jantac Cellars
P.O. Box 266
Palatine, IL 60078
(708) 397-7648

Leisure Time Pet & Hobby
123 S. Mattis
Country Fair Shopping Center
Champaign, IL 61821
(217) 352-4007

Lil' Olde Winemaking Shoppe
4 S. 245 Wiltshire Lane
Sugar Grove, IL 60554
(708) 557-2523

Old Town Liquors
514 S. Illinois Avenue
Carbondale, IL 62901
(618) 457-3513

You-Brew Country Food
  & Liquor
19454 S. Route 45
Mokena, IL 60448
(708) 479-2900

KANSAS

Ale-N-Vino
925 N. Kansas Avenue
P.O. Box 8155
Topeka, KS 66608
(913) 232-1990

Bacchus & Barleycorn
8725 Johnson Drive
Merriam, KS 66202-2150
(913) 262-4243

KENTUCKY

The Home Brewery
1446 N. 3rd Street
Bardstown, KY 40004
(800) 992-BREW
(502) 349-1001

Nuts N Stuff Bulk Foods
2022 Preston Street
Louisville, KY 40217
(502) 634-0508

Winemakers Supply & Pipe Shop
9477 Westport Road
Westport Plaza
Louisville, KY 40222
(502) 425-1692

LOUISIANA

The Beersmith
8158 Harry Drive
Baton Rouge, LA 70806
(504) 924-6544

MAINE

The Purple Foot Downeast
116 Main Street, Dept. Z
Waldoboro, ME 04572
(207) 832-6286

The Whip & Spoon
161 Commercial Street
P.O. Box 567
Portland, ME 04108
(800) 937-9447

MARYLAND

The Brewkeg
822-C Frederick Road
Cantonsville, MD 21228
(301) 747-2245

Brew Masters
12266 Wilkins Avenue
Rockville, MD 20852
(800) 466-9557

Cap & Cork
418 Essex Drive
Lexington Park, MD 20653
(301) 863-6721

CellarWorks at Fullerton Liquors
752 Belair Road
Baltimore, MD 21236
(410) 665-2900

The Flying Barrel
111 S. Carrol Street
Frederick, MD 21701
(301) 663-4491

MASSACHUSETTS

A & J Distributors
236 Hanover Street
Boston, MA 02113
(617) 523-8490
Fax (617) 720-5701

Barleymalt and Vine
4 Corey Street
Boston, MA 02132
(800) 666-7026

Barleymalt and Vine
280 Worcester Road
Framingham, MA 01701
(800) 666-7026

Beer and Wine Hobby
180 New Boston Street
Woburn, MA 01801
(617) 933-8818

Beer and Winemaking Supplies
154 King Street (Route 5)
Northampton, MA 01060
(413) 586-0150

The Brewers' Kettle
331 Boston Post Rd., Suite 12
Marlborough, MA 01572
(508) 485-2001

The Brew Shack
50 High Street
Amesbury, MA 01913
(508) 388-FOAM

The Modern Brewer Co.
2304 Massachusetts Avenue
Cambridge, MA 02140
(800) SEND-ALE
(617) 868-5580

Partners Village Store
999 Main Road
P.O. Box 3051
Westport, MA 02790
(508) 636-2572

The Vineyard-Home Brewers
and Vintners Supply
P.O. Box 80
Upton, MA 01568
(800) 626-2371
(508) 529-6014

MICHIGAN

The Barrel Shop
41 Courtland Street
Rockford, MI 49341
(800) 648-9860
(616) 866-3327

Diversions Beer &
Winemakers Supply
140 E. Front Street
Traverse City, MI 49684
(616) 946-6500

The Frankenmuth Brewery
Gift Shop
425 S. Main Street
Frankenmuth, MI 48734
(517) 652-2088

MINNESOTA

Brew-N-Grow
8179 University Avenue NE
Fridley, MN 55432
(612) 780-8191

MISSOURI

The Home Brewery
P.O. Box 730
Ozark, MO 65721-0730
(800) 321-BREW
(417) 485-0963

IMO Homebrew & Meadery
Supply
2901 Hallmark
P.O. Box 25485
Lemay, MO 63125
(314) 487-2130

St. Louis Wine & Beer Making
251 Lamp & Lantern Village
St. Louis, MO 63017
(314) 230-8277

Winemaker's Market
4349 N. Essex Avenue
Springfield, MO 65803
(314) 833-4145

NEVADA

Budgie Myster Home Brew Co.
2404 Howard Drive
Las Vegas, NV 89104
(702) 457-9671

The Home Brewery
4300 N. Pecos Road #13
N. Las Vegas, NV 89115
(800) 288-DARK
(702) 644-7002

NEW HAMPSHIRE

Brewer & Associates
Maine Hopper
112 State Street
P.O. Box 6555
Portsmouth, NH 04042

The Brewer's Basement
P.O. Box 521
Dover, NH 03820
(603) 749-2198

Granite State Natural Food, Inc.
164 North State Street
Concord, NH 03301
(603) 224-9341

Jasper's Home Brew Supply
11 D Tracy Lane
Hudson, NH 03051
(603) 881-3052

Orfordville Home Brew Supplies
Rt. 25A, RR1, Box 106A
Orford, NH 03777
(603) 353-4564

RCA Distributors
10 North Street
North Walpole, NH 03609
(603) 445-2018

NEW JERSEY

The Home Brewery
56 W. Main Street
Bogota, NJ 07603
(800) 426-BREW
(201) 525-1833

Red Bank Brewing Supply
67 Monmouth Street
Red Bank, NJ 07701
(908) 842-7507

Richland General Store
Rt. 40, P.O. Box 185
Richland, NJ 08350
(609) 697-1720

Wine Rack
293 Route 206
Flanders, NJ 07836
(201) 584-0333

NEW YORK

Arbor Wine & Winemaking
   Supplies
74 W. Main Street
East Islip, NY 11730
(516) 277-3004

Bottom of the Barrel
280 E. Dominick Street
Rome, NY 13440
(800) 437-3451
(315) 339-6744

The Brewery
11 Market Street
Potsdam, NY 13676
(800) 762-2560
(315) 265-0422

The Brewery Shop
830 Varick Street
Utica, NY 13502
(800) 765-6288

The Brews Brothers @ Kedko
564 Smith Street
Farmingdale, Long Island, NY 11735
(516) 454-7800

East Coast Brewing Supply
124 Jacques Avenue
P.O. Box 060904
Staten Island, NY 10306
(718) 667-4459
Fax (718) 987-3942

E.J. Wren Homebrewer
Ponderosa Plaza
209 Oswego Street
Liverpool, NY 13088
(315) 457-2282

Great South Bay Homebrew
   Supply
20 Bell Avenue
Blue Point, NY 11715
(516) 363-2407

Hennessy Homebrew, Inc.
470 N. Greenbush Road
Rensselaer, NY 12144
(518) 283-7094

The Homebrewers Connection
198 Smith Road
Spring Valley, NY 10977
(800) BREW123
(914) 368-8619

KEDCO - Beer & Wine
   Making Store
564 Smith Street
Farmingdale, NY 11735-2268
(800) 654-9988
(516) 454-7800

Little Shop of Hops
15 W. 39th Street
New York, NY 10018
(212) 704-4248
Fax (212) 704-9611

Little Shop of Hops
79 New Street
New York, NY 10004
(800) 343-HOPS

Mountain Malt & Hop Shoppe
93 Grove School Road
Catskill, NY 12414
(800) 295-MALT
(518) 943-2289

Mountain Malt & Hop Shoppe
54 Leggs Mills Road
Lake Katrine, NY 12449
(914) 336-7688

The New York Homebrew
36 Cherry Lane
Floral Park, NY 11001
(800) YOO-BREW
(516) 352-0878
Fax (516) 358-0587

Party Creations
RD 2, Box 35, Rokeby Road
Red Hook, NY 12571
(914) 758-0661

S&R Homebrewing &
    Winemaking Supplies
P.O. Box 5544, Union Station
Endicott, NY 13763
(607) 748-1877

U.S. Brewing Supply
815 Madison Avenue
Albany, NY 12208
(800) 383-9303
(518) 449-2470

NORTH CAROLINA

American Brewmaster
3021-7 Stoneybrook Drive
Raleigh, NC 27604
(919) 850-0095

NORTH DAKOTA

The Home Brewery
P.O. Box 1662
2215 Gateway Drive
Grand Forks, ND 58201
(800) 367-BREW
(701) 772-2671

OHIO

Homebrew-n-Stuff
1901-A Alex Road
W. Carrollton, OH 45449
(513) 866-4331

OKLAHOMA

Bob's Brewhaus
724 W. Cantwell Avenue
Stillwater, OK 74075
(405) 372-4477

OREGON

F.H. Steinbart
234 S.E. 12th Street
Portland, OR 97214
(503) 232-8793

Home Fermenter Center
123 Monroe Street
Eugene, OR 97402
(503) 485-6238

Wasson Bros. Winery & Beer
    and Wine Supply
41901 Highway 26
Sandy, OR 97055
(503) 668-3124

PENNSYLVANIA

Ambler Woodstove & Fireplace
Butler & Bethlehem Pikes
Ambler, PA 19002-6031
(215) 642-3565

Beer Unlimited
Routes 30 and 401
Great Valley Shopping Center
Malvern, PA 19355
(215) 889-0905

Bierhaus International
3723 West 12th Street
Erie, PA 16505
(814) 833-7747

BREW by YOU
3504 Cottman Avenue
Philadelphia, PA 19149
(215) 335-BREW

Country Wines
3333 Babcock Blvd
Pittsburgh, PA 15237-2421
(412) 366-0151

Home Sweet Homebrew
2008 Sansom Street
Philadelphia, PA 19103
(215) 569-9469

Spielgrund Gourmet Shop
3528 E. Market Street
York, PA 17402
(717) 755-3384

XYZed Music
Stone Mill Plaza
1386 Columbia Avenue
Lancaster, PA 17603
(717) 293-1214

RHODE ISLAND

Northeast Brewer's Supply
Mariner Square
140 Point Judith Rd., Unit C-45
Narragansett, RI 02882
(800) 352-9001

TENNESEE

Allen Biermakers
4111 Martin Mill Pike
Knoxville, TN 37920
(615) 577-2430

The Brewhaus
4955 Ball Camp Pike
Knoxville, TN 37921
(800) 638-2437
(615) 523-4615

Squash Blossom Market
5101 Sanderlin, Suite 124
Memphis, TN 38117
(901) 685-2293

TEXAS

Austin Homebrew Supply
306 E. 53rd Street
Austin, TX 78751
(512) 467-8427

DeFalco's Home Wine & Beer
  Supplies
5611 Morningside Drive
Houston, TX 77005
(800) 216-BREW
(713) 523-8154
Fax (713) 523-5284

Homebrew Headquarters
13929 N. Central Expwy.
Suite 449
Dallas, TX 75243
(214) 234-4411

The Winemaker Shop
5356 W. Vickery
Fort Worth, TX 76107
(800) TOP-BREW
(817) 377-4488
Fax (817) 732-4327

UTAH

Mountain Brew Retail
2793 S. State Street
S. Salt Lake City, UT 84115
(801) 487-2337

VERMONT

Something's Brewing
196 Battery Street
Burlington, VT 05401
(802) 660-9007

Vermont Homebrewer's Supply
Located at K&K Beverage
1341 Shelburne Road
South Burlington, VT 05403
(802) 985-9734

VIRGINIA

The Compleat Gourmet
3030 W. Cary Street
Richmond, VA 23221-3502
(800) 777-9606

Eats Natural Foods Co-op
1200 N. Main Street
Blacksburg, VA 24060
(703) 552-2279

Let's Brew
904 Chigwell Road
Virginia Beach, VA 23454-6549
(804) 721-3455

WASHINGTON

Brewer's Warehouse
4520 Union Bay Place N.E.
Seattle, WA 98105
(206) 527-5047

The Cellar Home Brew
14411 Greenwood N.
Seattle, WA 98133
(800) 342-1871
(206) 365-7660

Jim's 5-Cent Home Brew Supply
N. 2619 Division Street
Spokane, WA 99207
(800) 326-7769
(509) 328-4850

Liberty Malt Supply
1418 Western Avenue
Seattle, WA 98101
(206) 622-1880

Pike Place Brewery
1432 Western Avenue
Seattle, WA 98101
(206) 622-3373

West Seattle Homebrew Supply
4720 S.W. California Avenue
P.O. Box 16532
Seattle, WA 98116
(206) 938-2476

WEST VIRGINIA

Stone's Throw at Slight
 Indulgence
407 High Street
Morgantown, WV 26505
(304) 292-3401

Tent Church Vineyard
RD 1, Box 218
Colliers, WV 26035
(800) 336-2915
(304) 527-3916

WISCONSIN

Blues Brothers Brewing Supply
1733 Charles Street
La Crosse, WI 54603-2135
(608) 781-WINE

Hedtke's IGA Market
308 Clark Street
Hatley, WI 54440
(715) 446-3262

Life Tools Adventure Outfitters
1035 Main Street
Green Bay, WI 54301
(414) 432-7399

The Malt Shop
3211 N. Highway South
Cascade, WI 53011
(800) 235-0026
(414) 528-8697

The Market Basket
Homebrew & Wine Supplies
14835 W. Lisbon Road
Brookfield, WI 53005-1510
(414) 783-5233

North Brewery Supplies
9009 S. 29th Street
Franklin, WI 53132
(414) 761-1018

Nort's Worts
7625 Sheridan Road
Kenosha, WI 53143
(414) 654-2211

The Wine and Hop Shop
434 State Street
Madison, WI 53703
(608) 257-0099

APPENDIX FOUR

U.S. BREWPUBS AND MICROBREWERIES

(Note: Asterisk denotes brewpub)

ALASKA

Alaskan Brewing & Bottling Co.
P.O. Box 1053
Douglas, AK 99824
(907) 780-5866

Yukon Brewery
7851 Spring Street
Anchorage, AK 99518
(907) 349-7191

ARIZONA

Bandersnatch Brewpub*
125 E. 5th Avenue
Tempe, AZ 85281
(602) 966-4438

Barley's Brew Pub*
4883 North 20th Street
Phoenix, AZ 85016
(602) 468-0403

Crazy Ed's Black Mountain
   Brewing*
Box 1940
Cave Creek, AZ 85331
(602) 253-6293

Hops Restaurant and Brewery*
7000 E. Camelback Road
Scottsdale, AZ 85251
(602) 945-HOPS

San Francisco Bar &
   Grill Brewpub*
3922 N. Oracle
Tucson, AZ 85705
(602) 292-2233

CALIFORNIA

Alpine Village Hofbrau
833 W. Torrance Blvd, Street 4
Torrance, CA 90502

Anderson Valley Brewing Co.*
Buckhorn Saloon
14081 Highway 128
P.O. Box 505
Boonville, CA 95415
(707) 895-BEER

Angeles Brewing Co.
24921 Dana Point Harbor Drive
Dana Point, CA 92629
(714) 240-2060

Back Alley Brewery and Bistro*
5219 "G" Street
Davis, CA 95616
(916) 753-4571

Bay Brewing Co.
dba/Devil Mountain Brewery
850 South Broadway
Walnut Creek, CA 94596
(415) 935-2337

Belmont Brewing Co.
25 39th Place
Long Beach, CA 90803
(213) 433-3891

Bison Brewing Co.*
2598 Telegraph Avenue
Berkeley, CA 94704
(415) 841-7734

Boulder Creek Brewing
Boulder Creek Grill and Cafe
13040 Highway 9
Boulder Creek, CA 95006
(408) 338-7882

Brewhouse Grill Brewpub*
202 State Street
Santa Barbara, CA 93101
(805) 963-3090

Brewpub on the Green*
3350 Stevenson Blvd.
Fremont, CA 94538
(415) 651-5510

Brewski's Gaslamp Pub*
310 5th Avenue
San Diego, CA 92101
(619) 231-7700

Brown Street Brewery and
  Restaurant*
1040 Clinton St. at Brown St.
Napa, CA 94559
(707) 255-6392

Buffalo Bill's Brewery*
1082 B Street
Hayward, CA 94541
(415) 886-9823

Butterfield Brewery*
777 East Olive
Fresno, CA 93728
(209) 264-5521

Callahan's Pub & Brewery*
8280-A Mira Mesa Blvd.
San Diego, CA 92126
(619) 578-7892

Central Coast Brewing Co.
3432-A Roberto Court
San Luis Obispo, CA 93401
(805) 541-5883

Crown City Brewery*
300 S. Raymond Avenue
Pasadena, CA 91105
(818) 577-5548

Dempsey's Ale House/Sonoma
  Brewing Co.*
50 East Washington
Petaluma, CA 94952
(707) 765-9694

Etna Brewing Co.
131 Callahan Street
Etna, CA 96027
(916) 467-5277

Fullerton Hofbrau Brewery*
323 North State College Blvd.
Fullerton, CA 92631
(714) 870-7400

Golden Pacific Brewing Co. Inc.
5515 Doyle Street #4
Emeryville, CA 94608
(415) 655-3322

Gordon-Biersch Brewery
  Restaurant*
640 Emerson Street
San Francisco, CA 94301
(415) 323-7723
also at
33 E. San Fernando Street
San Jose, CA 95113
(408) 294-6785

Gordon-Biersch Brewing Co.*
2 Harrison Street
San Francisco, CA 94301
(415) 323-7723

Gorky's Russian Brewery*
576 E. 8th Street
Los Angeles, CA 90272
(213) 463-4060

Heritage Brewing*
24921 Dana Point Harbor Drive
Dana Point, CA 92629
(714) 240-2060

Hogshead Brewpub, Inc.*
114 J Street
Sacramento, CA 95814
(916) 443-BREW

Humboldt Brewery*
856 Tenth Street
Arcata, CA 95521
(707) 826-BREW

Huttenhain's Benicia Brewing*
321 First Street #5
Benicia, CA 94510
(408) 294-6785

J & L Brewing Co.
1945 Francisco Boulevard
East Suite Q
San Rafael, CA 94901
(415) 459-4846

Karl Strauss' Old Columbia
   Brewery and Grill*
1157 Columbia Street
San Diego, CA 92101
(619) 234-BREW

Kelmer's Brewhouse*
458 B Street
Santa Rosa, CA 95401
(707) 544-4677

La Jolla Brewing Co.*
7536 Fay Avenue
La Jolla, CA 92037
(619) 456-BREW

Lind Brewing Co.
1933 Davis Street #177
San Leandro, CA 94577
(510) 562-0866

Los Angeles Brewing Co. Inc.
1845 S. Bundy Drive
Los Angeles, CA 90272
(213) 459-4805

Lost Coast Brewery and Cafe*
617 4th Street
Eureka, CA 95501
(707) 445-4480

Mad River Brewing Co.
195 Taylor Way
Blue Lake, CA 95525
(707) 668-4151

Marin Brewing Co.*
1809 Larkspur Landing Circle
Larkspur, CA 94939
(415) 461-4677

Medicino Brewing*
Hopland Brewery Tavern
Box 400, 13351 S. Highway 101
Hopland, CA 95449
(707) 744-1015

Mission Brewing Co.
1751 Hancock Street
San Diego, CA 92110
(619) 298-7700

Monterey Brewing Co.*
638 Wave Street
Monterey, CA 94940
(408) 375-3634

Napa Valley Brewing Co. Inc.*
Calistoga Inn
1250 Lincoln Avenue
Calistoga, CA 94515
(707) 942-4101

North Coast Brewing Co.*
444 N. Main Street
Ft. Bragg, CA 95437
(707) 964-2739

Okie Girl Brewing*
658 Lebec Road
Lebec, CA 93243
(805) 248-6183

Pacific Coast Brewing Co.*
906 Washington Street
Oakland, CA 94607
(510) 836-2739

Red Kettle Fishery and Brewery*
131 Callahan Street
Etna, CA 96027
(916) 467-5277

Rubicon Brewing Company*
2004 Capitol Avenue
Sacramento, CA 95814
(916) 448-7032

Saint Stan's Brewery &
   Restaurant*
821 L Street
Modesto, CA 95354
(209) 524-BEER

San Andreas Brewing Co.*
737 San Benito Street
Hollister, CA 95023
(408) 637-7074

San Francisco Brewing Co.*
155 Columbus Avenue
San Francisco, CA 94133
(415) 434-3344

Santa Cruz Brewing Co.*
Front Street Pub
516 Front Street
Santa Cruz, CA 95060
(408) 429-8838

Seabright Brewery Inc.*
519 Seabright Avenue, #107
Santa Cruz, CA 95062
(408) 426-BREW

Sherwood Brewing*
319 Main Street
Chico, CA 95928
(916) 891-4502

Shields Brewing Co.*
24 East Santa Clara Street
Ventura, CA 93001
(805) 643-1807

Sierra Nevada Taproom &
   Restaurant*
1075 East 20th Street
Chico, CA 95928
(916) 345-2739

SLO Brewing Co. Inc.*
1119 Garden Street
San Luis Obispo, CA 93401
(805) 543-1843

Suderwerk, Privatbrauerei
   Hubsch*
2001 Second Street
Davis, CA 95616
(916) 756-2739

Tied House Cafe and Brewery*
954 Villa Street
Mountain View, CA 94041
(415) 965-2739
also at
65 N. San Pedro
San Jose, CA 95110

Triple Rock Brewing*
1920 Shattuck Avenue
Berkeley, CA 94704
(415) 843-2739

Truckee Brewing*
Pizza Junction
11401 Donner Pass Road
Truckee, CA 95734
(916) 587-7411

Twenty-Tank Brewery
316 11th Street
San Francisco, CA 94103
(415) 255-9455

Willett's Brewing Co. Inc.*
902 Main Street
Napa, CA 94559
(707) 258-2337

Winchester Brewing Co.*
820 S. Winchester Boulevard
San Jose, CA 95128
(408) 243-7561

COLORADO

Boulder Beer Company*
2880 Wilderness Place
Boulder, CO 80301
(303) 444-8448

Breckenridge Brewery and Pub*
800 South Main
Breckenridge, CO 80424
(303) 453-1550

Carvers Bakery Cafe Brewery*
1022 Main Street
Durango, CO 81301
(303) 259-2545

Champion Brewing*
1442 Larimer Square
Denver, CO 80202
(303) 534-5444

CooperSmith's Pub and
   Brewery*
No. 5 Old Town Square
Fort Collins, CO 80524
(303) 498-0483

The Hubcap Brewery and
   Kitchen*
143 East Meadow Drive
P.O. Box 3333
Vail, CO 81657
(303) 476-5757

Idle Spur Inc.*
dba/Crested Butte Brewery
   and Pub
226 Elk Avenue
P.O. Box 1089
Crested Butte, CO 81224

Oasis Brewery*
1095 Canyon Blvd.
Boulder, CO 80302
(303) 449-0363

Rock Bottom Brewery*
1001 16th Avenue
Denver, CO 80265
(303) 534-7616

San Juan Brewing Co.*
300 S. Townsend
P. O. Box 1989
Telluride, CO 81435
(303) 726-4587

The Walnut Brewery*
1123 Walnut
Boulder, CO 80302
(303) 447-1345

Wild Wild West Gambling Hall
and Brewery*
443 East Bennett
Cripple Creek, CO 80813
(719) 689-3736

Wynkoop Brewing Co.*
1634 18th Street
Denver, CO 80202
(303) 297-2700

CONNECTICUT

The Hartford Brewery Ltd.*
35 Pearl Street
Hartford, CT 06513
(203) 246-BEER

New England Brewing Co.
25 Commerce Street
Norwalk, CT 06851
(203) 866-1339

New Haven Brewing Co.
458 Grand Avenue
New Haven, CT 06513
(203) 772-2739

FLORIDA

Hops Grill & Brewery*
1451 US 19 South
Clearwater, FL 34624
(813) 531-5300

Hops Bar and Grill*
327 North Dale Mabry
South Tampa, FL 33609
(813) 871-3600

Market Street Pub*
120 Southwest 1st Avenue
Gainesville, FL 32601
(904) 377-2927

McGuires Irish Pub &
Brewery*
600 E. Gregory Street
Pensacola, FL 32501
(904) 433-6789

Mill Bakery, Eatery & Brewery*
65791 Newberry Road
Gainesville, FL 32605
(904) 331-1472
also at
2136 N. Moore
Tallahassee, FL 32303
(904) 386-2867
also at
330 West Fairbanks Avenue
Winter Park, FL 32789
(407) 644-1544

Sarasota Brewing Co.*
6607 Gateway Avenue
Sarasota, FL 34242
(813) 925-2337

IDAHO

Harrison Hollow Brewhouse*
2455 Harrison Hollow
Boise, ID 83702
(208) 343-6820

Table Rock Brewpub*
705 Fulton
Boise, ID 83702
(208) 342-0944

Treaty Grounds Brewpub*
W2124 Pullman Road
Moscow, ID 83843
(208) 882-3807

T.W. Fisher's Brewpub/Coeur
d'Alene Brewing Co.*
204 N. Second Street
Coeur D'Alene, ID 83814
(208) 664-BREW

ILLINOIS

Berhoff Brewery and Restaurant*
436 W. Ontario Street
Chicago, IL 60610
(312) 266-7771

Goose Island Brewing Co.*
1800 N. Clybourn
Chicago, IL 60613
(312) 915-0075

Joe's Brewing Co.*
706 South 5th
Champaign, IL 61820

Tap and Growler*
901 Jackson Boulevard
Chicago, IL 60607
(312) 829-4141

Weinkeller Brewery*
6417 W. Roosevelt Road
Berwyn, IL 60402
(708) 749-2276

INDIANA

Broad Ripple Brewing Co.*
840 East 65th Street
Indianapolis, IN 46220
(317) 253-2739

Mishawaka Brewing Co.*
3703 N. Main Street
Mishawaka, IL 46545
(219) 256-9994

IOWA

Dallas County Brewing/Old
    Depot Restaurant*
301 S. Tenth Street
Adel, Iowa 50003
(515) 993-5064

Fitzpatrick's Brewing Co.*
525 S. Gilbert Avenue
Iowa City, IA 52240
(319) 356-6900

Millstream Brewing*
P.O. Box 284
Lower Brewery Road
Amana, IA 52203
(319) 622-3672

KANSAS

Free State Brewing*
636 Massachusetts
Lawrence, KS 66044
(913) 843-4555

KENTUCKY

Oldenburg Brewing Co.*
I-75 at Buttermilk Pike
Fort Mitchell, KY 41017
(606) 341-2800

LOUISIANA

Crescent City Brewhouse*
527 Decatur Street
New Orleans, LA 70124
(504) 522-0571

Mill Bakery, Eatery & Brewery*
Essen Lane
Baton Rouge, LA 7084
(504) 769-1800

MAINE

Gritty McDuff's Brew Pub*
396 Fore Street
Portland, ME 04101
(207) 772-BREW

Lobster Deck Restaurant/
    Kennebunkport Brewing Co.*
8 Western Avenue
Kennebunk, ME 04101
(207) 967-4311

MARYLAND

Baltimore Brewing Co.
104 Albemarle Street
Baltimore, MD 21202
(410) 837-5000

Sisson's Restaurant/South Baltimore
Brewing Co.*
36 E. Cross Street
Baltimore, MD 21230
(301) 539-2093

MASSACHUSETTS

The Boston Beer Company
30 Germania Street
Boston, MA 02130
(617) 522-3400

The Boston Beer Works*
61 Brookline Avenue
Boston, MA 02115
(617) 536-2337

Cambridge Brewing Co.*
1 Kendall Square, Building 100
Cambridge, MA 02139
(617) 494-1994

The Commonwealth Brewing
    Co., Ltd.*
138 Portland Street
Boston, MA 02114
(617) 523-8383

John Harvard Brewhouse*
33 Dunster Street
Cambridge, MA 02113
(617) 868-3585

Northampton Brewery*
Brewster Court Bar & Grill
11 Brewster Court, P.O. Box 791
Northampton, MA 01061
(413) 584-9903

MINNESOTA
Sherlock's Home*
11000 Red Circle Drive
Minnetonka, MN 55361
(612) 931-0203

MISSOURI
The St. Louis Brewery/The
   Tap Room*
2100 Locust Street
Saint Louis, MO 63103
(314) 241-2337

MONTANA
Bayern Brewing*
Missoula Northern Pacific
North Higgins Avenue
Missoula, MT 59807
(406) 721-8705

NEBRASKA
Jaipur Restaurant and Brewpub*
10922 Elm Street
Omaha, NE 68144
(402) 392-7331

NEW MEXICO
Eske's A Brewpub*
Sangre de Cristo Brewing
P.O. Box 1572
Taos, NM 87571
(505) 758-1517

Preston Brewery*
Sangre de Cristo Brewing
Embudo Station Restaurant
P.O. Box 154
Embudo, NM 87531
(505) 852-4707

NEW YORK
Abbott Square Brewpub*
Buffalo Brewing
1830 Abbott Road
Buffalo, NY 14218
(716) 828-0004
also at
6861 Main Street
Williamsville, NY 14221
(716) 632-0552

Brown And Moran*
417-419 River Street
Troy, NY 12180
(518) 273-2337

Manhattan Brewing Co.
   Restaurant*
40-42 Thompson Street
New York, NY 10013
(212) 219-9250

Mountain Valley Brewpub*
122 Orange Avenue
Suffern, NY 10901
(914) 357-0101

Rochester Brewpub*
800 Jefferson Road
Henrietta, NY 14623
(716) 272-1550

Zip City Brewing*
3 West 18th Street
New York, NY 10011
(212) 366-6333

NORTH CAROLINA
Dilworth Brewing Co.*
1301 East Boulevard
Charlotte, NC 28203
(704) 377-2739

Greenshields Pub and Brewery*
214 E. Martin Street
Raleigh, NC 27601
(919) 828-0214

Loggerhead Brewing*
2006 W. Vandalia Road
Greensboro, NC 27407
(919) 292-7676

The Mill Bakery, Eatery and
Brewery*
12 West Woodland Road
Charlotte, NC 28217
(704) 529-6455

Old Heidelberg Village*
115 N. Duke Street
Durham, NC 27701
(919) 682-2337

Weeping Radish Brewery and
Restaurant*
Highway 64, P.O. Box 1471
Manteo, NC 27954
(919) 473-1157

OHIO

Columbus Brewing Co.*
476 Front Street
Columbus, OH 43215
(614) 224-3626

Great Lakes Brewing Co.*
2516 Market Street
Cleveland, OH 44113
(216) 771-4404

Hoster Brewing Co.*
550 S. High Street
Columbus, OH 43215
(614) 228-6066

Strongsville Brewing Co. dba/
Melbourne's Brewing Co.*
12492 Prospect Road
Strongsville, OH 44136
(216) 238-4677

OREGON

Bay Front Brewery & Public
House*
748 Bay Boulevard
Newport, OR 97365
(503) 265-3188

BridgePort Brewing Co. Inc.*
1313 N.W. Marshall
Portland, OR 97209
(503) 241-7179

Cornelius Pass Roadhouse and
Brewery*
4045 NW Cornelius Pass Road
Hillsboro, OR 97124
(503) 640-6174

Deschutes Brewery and Public
House*
1044 Bond Street NW
Bend, OR 97701
(503) 382-9242

Fulton Pub and Brewery*
0618 SW Nebraska Street
Portland, OR 97201
(503) 246-9530

High Street Pub*
1243 High Street
Eugene, OR 97401
(503) 345-4905

Highland Pub and Brewery*
4225 SE 182nd Avenue
Fresham, OR 97030
(503) 661-7538

Hillsdale Brewery and Public
House*
1505 SW Sunset Boulevard
Portland, OR 97201
(503) 246-3938

Hood River Brewing*
White Cap BrewPub
506 Columbia Street
Hood River, OR 97031
(503) 386-2247

Lighthouse Brew-Pub*
4157 N. Highway 101, Suite 117
Lincoln City, OR 97367
(503) 994-7238

McMenamin's*
6179 SW Murray Boulevard
Beaverton, OR 97005
(503) 644-4562

Oak Hills Brewpub*
14740 NW Cornell Road, Suite 80
Portland, OR 97229
(503) 645-0286

Pizza Deli and Brewery*
249 North Redwood Highway
144 Ken Rose Lane
Cave Junction, OR 97523
(503) 592-3556

Portland Brewing*
1339 NW Flanders Street
Portland, OR 97209
(503) 222-7150

Rogers Zoo*
2037 Sherman Avenue
North Bend, OR 97459
(503) 756-1463

Rogue Brewing Co. and Public
House*
31-B Water Street
Ashland, OR 97520
(503) 488-5061

Steelhead Brewery and Cafe*
199 East 5th Avenue
Eugene, OR 97401
(503) 485-4444

Thompson Brewery and Public
House*
3575 Liberty Road South
Salem, OR 97302
(503) 363-7286

Widmer Brewing Co.
B. Moloch - The Heathmen
Bakery and Pub*
901 SW Salmon
Portland, OR 97205
(503) 227-5700

PENNSYLVANIA

Allegheny Brewery & Pub*
Pennsylvania Brewing
800 Vinal Street
Pittsburgh, PA 15212
(412) 237-9400

Dock Street Brewing Co.
Brewery and Restaurant*
Two Logan Square
18th and Cherry Street
P.O. Box 30255
Philadelphia, PA 19103
(215) 496-0413

Samuel Adams Brewhouse*
Philadelphia Brewing
1516 Sansom Street, 2nd Floor
Philadelphia, PA 19102
(215) 563-ADAM

Stoudt Brewing Company*
Black Angus Restaurant
Rt. 272, P.O. Box 880
Adamstown, PA 19501
(215) 484-4387

SOUTH DAKOTA

Firehouse Brewing Co.*
610 Main
Rapid City, SD 57701
(605) 348-1915

UTAH

Eddie McStiff's*
57 South Main
Moab, UT 84532
(801) 259-BEER

Salt Lake Brewing Company*
Squatter's Pub Brewery
147 W. Broadway
Salt Lake City, UT 84101
(801) 363-BREW

Wasatch Brew Pub*
Schrif Brewing
250 Main Street
Park City, UT 84060
(801) 645-9500

VERMONT

The Vermont Pub and Brewery
of Burlington*
144 College Street
Burlington, VT 05401
(802) 865-0500

Windham Brewery*
6 Flat Street
Brattleboro, VT 05301
(802) 254-4747

VIRGINIA

Blue Ridge Brewing Co.*
709 West Main Street
Charlottesville, VA 22901
(804) 977-0017

19th Street Brewing*
1065 19th Street
Virginia Beach, VA 23451
(804) 491-5000

WASHINGTON

Big Time Brewing Company*
4133 University Way, NE
Seattle, WA 98105
(206) 545-4509

California and Alaska Brewery*
4720 California Avenue SW
Seattle, WA 98116
(206) 938-2476

Fort Spokane Brewery*
West 401 Spokane Falls Blvd.
Spokane, WA 99201
(509) 838-3809

Grant's Brewery Pub*
Yakima Brewing & Malting
32 North Front Street
Yakima, WA 90901
(509) 575-2922

Kirkland Roaster & Ale House*
Hales Ales
109 Central Way
Kirkland, WA 98033
(206) 827-4359

Pacific Northwest Brewing*
322 Occidental Avenue South
Seattle, WA 98104
(206) 621-7002

Redhook Ale Brewery*
Trolleyman's Pub
3400 Phinney Avenue N.
Seattle, WA 98103
(206) 548-8000

Thomas Kemper Brewing*
22381 Foss Road
Poulsbo, WA 98370
(206) 697-1446

WISCONSIN

Appleton Brewing Company*
Dos Bandidos Brew Pub
Johnny O's
1004 S. Olde Oneida Street
Appleton, WI 54915
(414) 735-0507

Brewmasters Pub*
Restaurant and Brewery
4017 80th Street
Kenosha, WI 53142
(414) 694-9050

Capital Brewery Co. Inc.*
7734 Terrace Avenue
P.O. Box 185
Middleton, WI 53562
(608) 836-7100

Cherryland Brewing Company*
341 North Third Avenue
Sturgeon Bay, WI 54235
(414) 743-1945

Fox Classic Brewing*
318 West College Avenue
Appleton, WI 54913
(414) 730-1166

Lakefront Brewery, Inc.*
818A East Chambers Street
Milwaukee, WI 53212
(414) 372-8800

Rowlands Calumet Brewing and
  Brewpub*
The Roll Inn
25 North Madison Street
Chilton, WI 53014
(414) 840-2534

Water Street Brewery*
1101 North Water Street
Milwaukee, WI 53202
(414) 272-1195

REFERENCE SOURCES

If you are interested in reading further, you may find this source list helpful. For specific topics, look for keyed items as follows:

Anderson, Will. *From Beer to Eternity*. Lexington, MA: The Stephen Greene Press, 1987.

Beer Judge Study Guide. Boulder, CO: The American Homebrewers Association, 1988.

Bradford, Daniel. "Lexicon of Beer Styles"; *Brewers Resource Directory* 1990-91. Boulder, CO: Brewers Publications, 1990.

Butcher, Alan D. *Ale and Beer: A Curious History*. Toronto, Ontario: M. Celland: Stewart, Inc., 1989.

Cox, Chuck. *Beer Judge Certification Exam Study Guide*. The Beer Judge Digest, 1992.

Doxat, John. *The Book of Drinking*. London: Triune Books, 1973.

Eckhardt, Fred. *The Essentials of Beer Style*. Portland, OR: Fred Eckhardt Associates, Second printing 1990. (5,6,7)

Finch, Christopher. *A Connoisseur's Guide to the World's Best Beer*. New York: Abbeville Press, 1989.

Forget, Carl. *Dictionary of Beer and Brewing*. Boulder, CO: Brewer Publications, 1988. (3,5,6)

Grossman, Harold J. *Grossman's Guide to Wine, Spirits, and Beers*. New York, NY: Charles Scribner and Sons, 1964.

Jackson, Michael. *The New World Guide to Beer*. Philadelphia, PA: Running Press, 1988, reprinted 1989. (5,6,7,8)

Jackson, Michael. *Pocket Guide to Beer*. New York, NY: Simon & Schuster, 1991.

Jackson, Michael. "Can Belgium's Rodenbach Survive?" *Zymurgy*. Boulder, CO: American Homebrewers Association, Fall 1991.

Mazer Cup Mead Competition, 1992 enrollment information.

Miller, Dave. *Brewing The World's Great Beers*. Pownal, VT: Storey Communications, 1991 (1-800-441-5700).

Miller, Dave. *The Complete Handbook of Home Brewing*. Pownal, VT: Storey Communications, Eighth Printing, 1991 (1-800-441-5700). (2,3,4,5,6,8)

Morris, Stephen. *The Great Beer Trek.* Brattleboro, VT: The Stephen Greene Press, 1987.

Papazian, Charlie. *The New Complete Joy of Home Brewing.* New York, NY: Avon Press, Second Edition, 1991. (2,3,5,8)

Prokesch, Steven. "Small British Brewers Make a Dent." New York Times, NY: November 28, 1991.

Robertson, James D. *The Great American Beer Book.* New York, New York: Warner Books, reissued 1981. (1)

Willenbecher, James F. *Conconction or a Beer Engineer.* Broad Brook, CT: OEI Publications, 1992.

Zymurgy Special Issue — 1985 "Grain Brewing." Boulder, CO: American Homebrewers Association, 1985.

Zymurgy Special Issue — 1987 "Trouble-shooting." Boulder, CO: American Homebrewers Association, 1987. (4)

Zymurgy Special Issue — 1989 "Yeast and Beer." Boulder, CO: American Homebrewers Association, 1989. (3,8)

Zymurgy Special Issue — 1990 "Hops and Beer." Boulder, CO: American Homebrewers Association, 1990.

Zymurgy Winter Issue — 1991 "Beer from Water." Boulder, CO: American Homebrewers Association, 1991.

Zymurgy Spring Issue — 1991 "Traditional Beer Styles." Boulder, CO: American Homebrewers Association, 1991. (6)

GLOSSARY

Acrospire. The embryonic barley plant which grows inside the husk during germination.

Adjunct. Any unmalted grain used as a source of sugar in brewing.

Ale. Beer made with ale yeast *(Saccharomyces cerevesia)*, often with a fruity aroma caused by fermenting at warmer temperatures.

Alpha Acid. A sticky, bitter resin found in hops, which imparts bitterness to the finished beer.

Amylase. Any enzyme which breaks the bonds that hold starch molecules together.

Appearance. The overall look of a particular beer sample.

Aroma. The smell produced by the raw ingredients, not the bittering compounds, in beer.

Aroma Hops. Hops used to impart aroma, as opposed to bitterness, to beer.

Aromatic Hops. Hops varieties known for their fine aroma and flavoring properties. Also known as Noble hops.

Attenuation. The drop in specific gravity that takes place as the wort ferments.

Autolysis. A process in which starving yeast cells feed on each other by excreting enzymes; causes an unpleasant rubbery stench in beer.

Bacteria. Primitive microorganisms smaller than yeast. Certain types of bacteria can infect wort and beer and result in off-flavors.

Beta Acid. A soft, bitter hop resin; harsher in flavor than alpha acid, but almost insoluble at normal wort pH values.

Bittering Hops. Hops added to the wort early in the boil to cause bitterness.

Body. The sensation of fullness or viscosity in the mouth, imparted by malt proteins in beer. See also Mouthfeel.

Bottle-conditioned. Carbonated by a second fermentation that takes place in the bottle as a result of yeast left in the mixture after bottling.

Bottle-fermenting. Describes yeasts that flocculates late in the fermentation and sinks to the bottom of the fermenter.

Break. Visible particles of protein and other matter that form in wort during boiling and cooling.

Brewing. The process of making wort, boiling it with hops and fermenting it into beer.

Carbonation. The process of dissolving carbon dioxide gas in a liquid, such as beer.

Cold Break. The flocculation of protein and polyphenol molecules during wort cooling.

Chill Haze. Tiny particles that form in beer when it is chilled and make the beer appear cloudy. An undesirable characteristic.

Clarifier. A substance used to remove or prevent chill haze.

Conversion. The process in which natural malt enzymes change grain starch into sugar during the mash.

Decoction. A method of mashing which boosts temperature from one step to the next by removing a portion of the mash, boiling it, and returning it to the main brew kettle.

Dextrins. Complex carbohydrates that contribute to the mouthfeel of beer.

Diacetyl. A compound that gives beer a butterscotch-like taste.

Diastatic Power. A measure of the total amylase content of a given sample of malt; usually expressed in degrees Lintner.

Dimethyl Sulfide (DMS). A powerful aromatic compound which imparts a sweet creamed corn smell to lager mashes. In finished beer it imparts a malty quality, or, at higher levels, the taste of cooked vegetables.

Dry. Opposite of sweet. In a dry beer, bitterness predominates over sweetness.

Endosperm. The nonliving part of the barley grain, which contains starch and protein to feed the growing acrospire.

Enzyme. A complex protein which has the ability to form or break a particular chemical bond.

Esters. A class of compounds formed by joining an alcohol and an acid; many have powerful fruity aromas.

F. Abbreviation for Fahrenheit, the scale used to measure temperature in the United States.

Fermentation. The metabolism of sugar into carbon dioxide and alcohol, performed by yeast and some bacteria.

Fermenter. A vessel used to contain wort during fermentation.

Finings. Any substance used to help yeast flocculate and settle out after fermentation.

Finishing Hops. Hops added to the wort late in the boil, to impart a hoppy aroma rather than bitterness.

Flocculation. The process in which yeast cells clump together to form large visible particles, which can then fall out of suspension.

Grist. The crushed malts and adjuncts that are mixed with hot water to from the mash.

Haze. An undesirable cloudiness in beer, caused by tine particles that form in the beer during chilling. See also Chill haze.

High-Alpha Hops. Hops varieties bred primarily for maximum bittering power. These are most useful as bittering hops.

Hops. The cones or flowers of the female *Humulus lupulus* plant. They may be dried whole hops, or may be used after being dried into pellets.

Hot Break. The flocculation of protein and polyphenol molecules during boiling.

IBU. International Bittering Units. A standard measure of the hop content in beer.

Infection. The growth of any microorganism in wort or beer, except for the brewer's yeast that was deliberately added. Most infections harm the flavor of the finished product.

Infusion. Single-vessel heating used to breakdown the stored starches within the grain into fermentable sugars.

Isomerization. The extraction of hop bitterness.

Lactic Acid. A tart acid, produced by yeast and by certain types of bacteria that infect beer.

Lager. Beer that is fermented cool using lager yeast *(Saccharomyces carlsbergensis)* and stored cold for a period of weeks in order to give it a clean, smooth flavor. From the German verb meaning "to store."

Lauter Tun. A vessel used to strain the sweet liquor or wort off the spent grains after mashing.

Lovibond. The scale, in degrees, on which American brewers measure the color or malt, wort, and occasionally the color of beer.

Lupulin Glands. The tiny yellow sacs found at the base of the petals of the hop cone. They contain the alpha acids, beta acids, and hop oils.

Malt. Barley or other grain which has been soaked with water, allowed to sprout, and then dried. Sprouting allows development of the enzymes that bring about starch conversion in the mash.

Mash. 1. (verb) To make a thick mixture of hot water with crushed malt and, in some cases, adjuncts, in which the grain starches are converted to sugar. 2. (noun) The mixture described in definition number one.

Mouth feel. The sensation of fullness in the mouth, created by dextrins and proteins in the beer. See also Body.

Original Gravity. The specific gravity of the wort before fermentation begins.

Oxidation. Any chemical reaction involving oxygen. It gives beer an undesirable flavor.

pH. The measure of acidity or alkalinity. 7 is the neutral point of the scale, with lower values being acid, and higher values alkaline.

Phenolic. Any compound based on a ring of six carbon atoms joined by alternating single and double bonds. The so-called tannins contained in grain husks are phenolic in nature, as are the soft hop resins, also called alpha and beta acids.

Polyphenols. Complex compounds based on two or more phenolic rings joined together.

Protein. Any complex organic compound containing nitrogen.

Rack. To transfer beer from one vessel to another, leaving the sediment behind.

Reinheitsgebot. German Purity Law allowing only water, malted barley, malted wheat, hops, and yeast to be used in the brewing of beer.

Respiration. The process in which living things oxidize sugar in order to obtain energy.

Sanitize. To make clean and free of microorganisms.

Sparge. To rinse the grain bed in the lauter tun with hot water in order to recover the residual sugar.

Specific Gravity. A measure of density. This measurement compares the heaviness of a given volume of beer to pure water. Malt sugar increases the specific gravity of wort and fermentation (by removing the sugars) lowers it. The scale is absolute, meaning a specific gravity of 1.050 means the beer weighs 1.05 times as much as an equal amount of water.

SRM. Standard Research Method. A standard measurement of the color range of a specific beer or style of beer.

Strain. Yeast which shares a common genetic makeup and specific traits, such as flavoring properties.

Style. The whole sum of flavor and other sensory characteristics by which individual beers may be placed in categories for purposes of comparison, tasting, and judging. Beers of the same style have the same general flavor profile.

Terminal Gravity. The specific gravity of beer after fermentation is completed. Also called final gravity.

Top-fermenting. Describes yeast that flocculates relatively early in this fermentation and is carried up into the head of foam in the wort by carbon dioxide bubbles.

Wild Yeast. Any yeast that is introduced accidentally into wort or beer from the environment.

Wort. A sugar solution derived from grain by mashing and sparging.

Yeast. A relatively large and complex single-celled microorganism. It thrives on sugar, which it ferments, but also requires oxygen and other nutrients in order to grow.

INDEX

Page numbers in **boldface** refer to charts.
Page numbers in *italics* refer to illustrations.

Degrees Lintner, 82
Delbruck, Max, 78
Density, of the wort, 18, 20
Dextrins, in beer, 20, 128
Diacetyl flavor, 68, 77, 128
Diastatic malt, 13
Diastatic power, measurement of, 82, 128
Diet/lite lagers, American, 40, **52**
DMS (Dimethyl sulfide), sweet corn flavor of, 66, 68, 70, 74, 128
Doppelbock, 46–47, **52**
Dortmunder Beer, 43, **52,** 72–73
Draft ales, 39
Dreher, Anton, 43
Dry, definition of, 128
Dry beers, American, 41
Drying, malt, 10
Dry Stout, 37, **58**
Dunkel Weizen beer, 27, **54**

Egypt, records of early brewing, 3
Eisbock, 47, **54**
Embryo, as growing part of grain, 9, 81
Endosperms, during grain germination, 9–10, 81, 128
English ales
    Brown ale, 35, **58,** 72
    Old Ale (Strong Ale), 38–39
    Pale ale, 33, **58,** 72
    types of hops used, **85**
Enzymes
    definition, 128
    in kilned malts, 10, 12
    in wheat, 82
Epsom salt, effect on water, 71
Esters
    flavor of, 68
    fruity aromas of, 66, 76, 128
    as yeast byproducts, 76, 78
Examination, for certification as beer judge, 98–100, 102–4

Faro beer, 29
Fermentation, role of yeast, 4, 6, *11,* 19–22, 128, 130
Filter bed, husk as, 9, 80
Filtration process, *11,* 23
    sediments in homebrews, 63
Finishing hops, 16, 128
Flanders brown beer, 31, **56**
Flashlight, for beer judging, 88, 97, 103
Flavor
    added by hops, 17, 74
    imparted by roasted grains, 13
    judging, 67–70, 93–95
    role of husk in, 9
Flemish beer, early use of hops in, 4–5
Flocculation, 16, 128

Fluorescent lights, effect on bottled beers, 66
Foam, appearances of, 63–64
Food, aftertaste effect on beer judging, 88, 103
Foreign Stout, 37, **58**
Fox beer, 28
Fructose, fermentation by yeast, 21
Fruit beers. *See* Lambic beers
Fruitiness, in specific beers, 27, 76–77
Fruity taste, of ales, 28, 30, 33, 65, 68, 127
Fungi, as source of moldy flavor, 70
Fusel oils in alcohol, 66, 67

Gall, Saint, 4
Gas release, in judged beers, 92
Gelatin, as clarifying agent, 79
German ales, 25–28
German Pilsner, 42–43, **52**
Germination process, 9–10
    scenario for, 1–2
Glass-making technology, effect on enhancing lager beer, 6
Glassware, use in judging beer, *2,* 86–87
Glucose, fermentation by yeast, 20
Goat, as bock beer symbol, 46
Grains
    milling of, 13–14, 68
    storage in brewhouses, 8
    use in brewing, 80–84, **83**
Grain wine (Sikaru), as name for Babylonian beer, 3
Grainy flavor, 68
Grassy flavor, 70
Gravity
    benefits in brewing process, 8
    final, 130
    original, **52–60,** 129
Green apple flavor, 70
Green malt, 10
Grist, 128
Gueuze beer, 28
Guilds, brewers', 5
Gushing, in bottled beers, 63
Gyle (priming malt), 24
Gypsum, effect on water, 71, 72

Hafnia protea, bacterial infection, 66, 68, 74
Hansen, Emil, 6, 78
Hardness, water, minerals effecting, 71–72
Haze
    effect of cold aging on, 40, 128
    husk as contributing factor, 82
    in judged beers, 91
    minimizing during brewing process, 9–0, 13, 16, 18
    in specific beers, 26
    types of, 64–65, 80, 84
Head, beer, appearances of, 63–64, 92–93

Head space, in bottled beers, 62–63, 91
Heat exchanger, *11*
Hefe-weizen beer, 27, **54**
Helles Bock, 46, **52**
Herbed beers, 49
Hieroglyphics, depicting brewing, 3
High alpha hops, 75, 76, 128
High gravity beers, esters in, 66
High-kilned lager malts, 12
Hippocras mead, 51
Homebrews
    judging, 89, 90, 97–98
    sediments in, 63
Home Wine and Beer Trade Association
    (HWBTA), certification of beer judges,
    98–99
Honey, use in mead, 51
Honorary Master certification, **99**
Hop back (hop jack) strainer, 18
Hop nose, judging by smell, 65
Hoppiness, taste of, 67
Hops, *11*
    addition during boiling process, 17–18
    early use in brewing, 4–5
    finishing, 16, 128
    IBU rankings, 25, **53–61**
    noble, 28, 76
    taste of in beer judging, 94
    varieties of, 74–76, **77, 85,** 128
Hot break process, during boiling stage, 16–18, 129
Humulus lupulus. See Hops
Husk, grain, during brewing process, 9, 13, 73, 80–81
HWBTA. *See* Home Wine and Beer Trade Association
Hydrogen, use of calcium to release in water, 73
Hydrogen sulfide (H_2S), effect on flavor, 70
Hydrometers, 18–19, 22

IBU (International Bittering Units), 25, 40–41, **53–61,** 129
Ice technique, use in Eisbock, 47
Imperial Stout, 38, **60**
India Pale Ale (IPA), 34, 48, **58**
Infections, signs of, 63, 65, 66, 68, 69, 91, 129
Infusion method, *11*, 15, 129
Ingredients, brewing, as allowed under German purity laws, 5–6
Institute for Brewing and Fermentation Studies (Berlin), 78
International Bittering Units (IBU), 25, **53–61,** 129
Ions, water, effect on brewing, 71, 73
Irish Moss (Copper fining), as clarifying agent, 79
Isinglass, as clarifying agent, 79

Isomerization, 17, 129

Jacobsen, Jacob Christian, 78
Jean I (Duke of Brabant), 5
Judges, role in taste tests, 95–98

Kegging, *11*, 24
Kettles, brew, 16, 17, 68
Kilning process, 10, 12–13
King of Beer, Jean I as, 5
Kit, judging, 97
Kloeckera apiculata (brewing yeast), 78
Knights of the Mashing Fork, 5
Kolsch beer, 26, **54**
Krausening method, of priming, 24
Kriek beer, types of hops used, **85**

Lactic acid, 129
Lactobacillus delbrueckii (brewing yeast), 78
Lactose (milk sugar), in Sweet stout, 38
Lager
    comparison of beers, 40–42
    fermentation, 6, 19, 129
    malts, 10, 12
    types of hops used, **85**
    yeast, 78
Lagering, as German storage method, 5
Lag phase, of fermentation, 19–20
Lambic beers, 21–22, 28, 49, **56,** 78
Lautering phase, role of husk, 9, 80
Lauter tun, use in heating process, *11*, 15–16, 129
Laying-down beers, 38–39
Light beer, American, 6–7
Lighting, effect on beer judging, 88
Light-Struck (skunked), characteristic of bottle beers, 66
Linter, measurement system, 82
London, Eng., effect of water on ales, 72
Lovibond scale, malt colors, 84, 129
Lupulin gland, hops, 17–18, 74, 129

Magnesium, use to lower pH, 73
Magnesium sulfate ($MgSO_4$), effect on water, 71
Malt, 1–2, 129
    processing, 9–13
    taste of, 67, 94
    types of, 10, 12, **83**
Malt beers
    American, 42
    size of head and bubbles, 63–64
Malt extract, use in priming process, 24
Maltose, fermentation by yeast, 20–21
Marston brewery (Eng.), 21–22
Marzen (Oktoberfest) Beer, 44, **52**
Mashed malts, 12, 129

Mashing process, 14–16, 80, 129
Mash tun, *11*, 14, *15*
Meads, 21, 50–51
Medicine chest flavor, 67
Mediterranean area, as cradle of beer brewing, 1–3
Melanoidins, creation of, 17
Melomel mead, 51
Mesopotamia, early beer brewing, 3
Metallic flavor, 68
Methegiln mead, 51
Microbrewers, 7, 84–85
Mild ale malts, 10, 12
Mild Brown ale, 35, **58**
Milk Stout (Sweet Stout), 37–38, **60**
Milk sugar (lactose), in Sweet stout, 38
Milling process, 13–14
Minerals, water, effect on brewing, 71
Moisture content, during steeping, 9
Moldy flavor, 70
Monks, as first researchers, 4
Mouth feel, in judging beers, 67, 90, 93–94
    conditioning before exam, 102-3
Multi-level designs, of brewhouses, 8, *11*
Munich, Ger., carbonated water at, 72
Munich Dunkel beer, 45, **52**
Munich Helles beer, 44–45, **52**
Munich Malt, 12

Near-beer, 7
New England-style cider, 50
Nin-Bi, as goddess of brewing, 3
Nitrate, presence of, 74
Noble hops (Aromatic hops), 28, 76, 127
Nutty flavor, 69

Oatmeal Stout, 38, **60**
Oats, **83**
Off-flavors, minimizing of, 9, 73, 79
Oils, from hops, 17–18, 74, 76
Oktoberfest (Marzen) Beer, 44, **52**
Organizers, beer judgings, 100–101
Original gravity, **52-60,** 129
Oxidation, 10, 129
Oxidized flavor, 69
Oxygen, role in fermentation, 20

Pale ales, 22, 33, 34, 48, **56, 58**
Pale malts, 10, 12, 14, 84
Pasteur, Louis, 6
Paulaner Brewery (Ger.), 47
Permanent hardness, water, 72
Phenolic
    definition, 129
    flavor, 67–68
    odors, 66
pH factor, 14, 73, 82, 129
Phytase enzyme, 14–15

Pictograms, of early beer brewing, 3
Pilsner beers, 42–43, **52**
    water for, 72
Pilsner Urquell, 42, **53**
Pitching process, of yeast, 19, 20, 22
Polyclar, as clarifying agent, 80
Polyphenols, 13, 14, 82, 129
Porter
    appearance of head, 63
    hops used, **85**
    types of, 36–37, **58**
Pouring, during beer judgings, 90–91
Premium beers, American, 40–41
Preservative, role of hops, 5, 74
Priming materials, in final stages, 23–24
Prohibition era, American, 7
Proteins, 16, 19, 129
Proteolytic enzymes, 14
Purity, beers, German laws for, 5–6
Pyment mead, 51
Pyruvic acid, as precursor of alcohol, 20

Racking process, 22–23, 63, 129
Raspberries, use in lambic beers, 49
Raspberry syrup, 27
Rauchbier, 45, **54**
"Rauchenfels" beer, 22
Recipe, beer, Sumerian pictographs of, 3
"Reinheitsgebot of 1516", as beer purity law, 5–6, 129
Residue, in bottled beers, 63
Resins, from hops, 74, **75**
Respiration phase, of fermentation, 20, 130
Retention, head, 64
Rice, **83**
Rice wine, 49
Roasting grains method, 12–13
Robust Porter, 36, **58**
Rollers, settings for milling, 13
Rolling boil process, 16–17, 84
Roman Catholic Church, role in early beer brewing, 4
Rome, ancient, introduction of beer to Europe, 3

Saccharomyces cerevisia (brewing yeast), 76–77
Saccharomyces delbrueckii (brewing yeast), 78
Saccharomyces uvarum (*S. carlsbergensis*) (brewing yeast), 77–78, 129
St. Francis Paula abbey (Ger.), 47
Saison beer, 30, **56**
Sake, 49–50
Salty flavor, 69
Samuel Smith's Brewery (Eng.), 22
Sanitation process, 69, 130
Schwartzbier, 45, **52**

Scottish ales, strong, **32,** 33, **56**
Sedelmayer, Gabriel, 6, 44, 78
Sediment, in bottled beers, 63, 91
Sherry-like flavor, 69
"Shilling" designation, Scottish ales, **32,** 33, 39
Sikaru (Grain wine), of Babylonia, 3
Six-row barley, 81, 84
Smoke, effect on beer judging, 88
Smoked-type beers, 45, 49
Sodium chloride, use for smoothness, 73
Solubility, of hop resins, 17
Solvent flavor, 69
Sour flavor, 69, 73
Sparging process, for recovering sugar liq uid, 16, 130
Sparkling cider, 50
Speciality cider, 50
Speciality grains, use to impart distinct fla vors, 12
Specific gravity, 18, 22–23, 130
Standard beers, American, 40, **52**
Standard Research Method (SRM), ranking of beer colors, 25, **52-60,** 84, 130
Star, as beer-brewing symbol, 4
Starches, breaking down, 2, 10, 15, 82
Steam beer (California Common Beer), 47–48, **54, 85**
Steeping process, 9
Stein beer
    fermenting process, 22
    types of hops used, **85**
Stewards, role in beer judgings, 96, 101
Stewed malts, 12
Still cider, 50
Storage, grain, in brewhouses, 8
Stout
    appearance of head, 63, 92
    types of, 37–38, **58, 60**
Strain, yeast, 130
Strong Ale (English Old Ale), 38–39
Style profiles, of beers, 35–61, 90, 102, 130
Sucrose, fermentation by yeast, 20
Sugars, 20–21, 38
    breakdown of, 2, 15–16, 82
Sulfate, use in achieving taste, 74
Sulphury flavor, 70
Sumeria, first beer recipe, 3
Sunlight, effect on bottled beers, 66
Sweet flavor, 69
Sweet liquor. *See* Wort
Sweet Stout (Milk Stout), 37–38, **60**

Tannins
    during hot break process, 16
    in husks, 9, 13, 15, 82–83
Taste, of judged beers, 90, 93–95
Temperature

for fermentation processes, 19
    during kilning process, 10
    recommended for judged beers, 90–91
Temporary hardness, water, compounds in, 72
Terminal gravity, 130
Time of day, for beer judging, 88
Tongue, distinguishing flavors with, 93, **94**
Top-fermenting yeast, 130
Touch, role in judging beers, 93
Trappist (abbey) ales, 29–30, **56**
Two-row barley, 81

Vienna Beer, 43, **52**
Vienna Malt, 12
Volsted Act of 1919, 7

Water
    for brewing, 9, 13, 14, 15
    density of, 22
    drinking during beer judging, 89
    as ingredient in beer, 71–74
Water-softening equipment, 72
Weizen (Weissbier) beer, 26, **54,** 78
Weizenbock beer, 27–28, **54**
Wheat, use as brewing grain, 81–82
Wheat beers
    appearance of head, 63, 81–82, 92
    types of hops used, **85**
Whirlpool process, *11,* 18
Wild yeast, 2, 79, 130
William VI (Elector of Bavaria), 5
Wine glasses, use in judging beer, 87
Wit (White) beer, 28, **56**
Woodruff syrup, 27
Wort, *11*
    adding yeast to, 19
    during the boiling stage, 16, 17
    cooling process, 18–19
    making, 16, 130
    reduction of gravity, 20
    use in priming process, 24

Yeast, *11,* 130
    addition during cooling process, 18
    ale, 66
    autolysis effect on flavor, 70
    pitching, 19, 20, 22
    processing in Burton Union system, 21
    quality and bottle sediment, 63
    role in fermentation, 4, 19–22
    strain, 130
    top-fermenting, 130
    types of, 76–79
    wild, 2, 79, 130
Yeast, wine, use in apple juice cider, 50
Yorkshire Stone Square, fermentation sys tem, 22